Praise for **The Inside Game: Sales Basics**

"Mark Shriner is one of the best sales people I've ever met. His book, *The Inside Game: Sales Basics* provides a ton of useful information about the art and skill of successful of selling."

Will Linssen, Practice Leader Asia & EMEA for Marshall Goldsmith Stakeholder Centered Coaching

"Smart. Lively. A must-read for everyone who is serious about sales – from entrepreneur to every manager who is interested in growing sales."

Virginia Chan, Co-founder of Compare Clinic

"Sales fundamentals for both beginners and professionals alike. Explained in step-by-step approach understandable to all. Great reading!"

Pete Helin, Senior Vice President Supply Chain, Enics AG

"Mark`s book is straight to the point and easy to read. It covers the basics in sales and not only gets you started but turns you into a top performer."

Anja Birkelbach, Sales Trainer PwC

"What "*The Inside Game: Sales Basics*" does differently is present its arguments in a very down to earth and highly readable format. It caters not only for someone starting out in sales but also serves as a great refresher for an experienced sales professional. I recommend it as a comprehensive guide to high performance sales."

Guy Day, Chief Operating Officer, Eames Consulting Group

"Sales is the lifeblood of any organization, more so for startups. Hence "sales basics" is exactly what they need to help them commercialize their brilliant technical ideas. This book provides many pointers that they can work on and master."

R Subramaniam Iyer, Chairman, Apple Seed Pte Ltd.

"A down to earth sales manual offering practical techniques on all stages of the sale process. A good tool for new salespeople, and serves as a reminder for more senior salespeople of the things we sometimes forget."

Mike Hay, President Ringier Trade Media

"A well thought out coverage of sales fundamentals by a seasoned professional with a large amount of international exposure. Relying on actionable advices, Mark Shriner delivers a straightforward "learning by doing" compendium…and really enjoyable reading!"

Jean-Philippe Lopez, Director of Business Development Global Industrial Affairs for Sanofi

The Inside Game

Sales Basics

Mark Shriner

www.theinsidegame-sales.com

Copyright © 2014 by Mark Shriner. All rights reserved. Printed in the United States of America. Except as permitted under the United States Copyright Act of 1976, no part of this publication may be reproduced or distributed in any form or by any means, or stored in a database or retrieval system, without the prior written permission of the author and the publisher.

ISBN 150231147X

For information regarding bulk sales:
admin@theinsidegame-sales.com

To my family, friends, colleagues, and clients

Contents

Introduction	1
Knowledge and Belief	9
Targeting	15
Prospecting	23
Get the Meeting!	31
Directing the Meeting	43
Effective Presentations	55
Features vs. Benefits	71
Understanding Your Prospect	85
The Importance of Trust	93
Consultative Selling	101
Closing Made Easy	115
Lead Generation	131
The Importance of Motivation	153

Continual Development	167
Effective Use of CRM Tools	175
How to become a top performing sales person and enjoy every step of the way!	189
The Quickest Way to Become a Sales Superstar; Walk the Walk	199
TEN SECRETS OF SALES SUPERSTARS	209
Acknowledgments	215
About the Author	217

Introduction

"The minute you get away from fundamentals – whether its proper technique, work ethic or mental preparation – the bottom can fall out of your game, your schoolwork, your job, whatever you're doing." - Michael Jordan

Do you want to sell more? Do you want to make more money than you ever have before? Do you want to become a sales superstar and have fun while you are at it?

If so, then this is the book for you! Why? Because this book will teach you the "secrets" of successful sales. Those "secrets" are the foundation of all successful sales careers, and are what many people ironically call "the basics."

With so many different books and courses on the market covering an incredibly diverse array of "advanced," "new and improved", and "revolutionary" sales techniques and methods, why would anyone want to read, let alone write a book on a seemingly mundane subject such as "sales basics?"

Well, as Michael Jordan has stated above, the fundamentals or basics are the foundation for "whatever you're doing." They play an important role in your success in any arena. To ignore the basics is to court failure.

If you look at star athletes, musicians, entertainers, and business people, they all have started their careers by developing and emphasizing the fundamentals of whatever activity they are pursuing.

We have all heard stories of star performers such as David Beckham kicking corner kicks over and over, day after day, week after week, month after month, and year after year until he could make the ball do what he wanted without conscious thought. We know stories of professional musicians who practice simple scales for hours at a time, or actors who do basic acting exercises to prepare for performances.

What, you may ask, do these stories have to with sales? Sales isn't really an athletic or musical activity, is it? And salespeople aren't performers, are they?

In fact, salespeople are performers, in both senses of the word. They perform their role of selling, i.e. generating sales for their company. And whenever they are in front of client, they are playing the part of a trusted advisor in a genuine, believable, and effective manner, so that the people they are doing business with will trust them and their service or product.

This is easier said than done. The fundamentals for some activities may involve a few different physical and mental activities. Some martial arts, for example, only have a few basic stances, punches, and kicks. Of course, mastery of these techniques can take years of practice. But because the number of fundamentals is relatively few, it may be easier for practitioners to focus on those key techniques and remember them when performing.

Sales, on the other hand, is a relatively complex activity. There are so many different dynamics involved and intertwined with sales and the sales process that it can be easy to lose sight of or even forget some of the basics. I mean, in sales, we are dealing with the most complex phenomenon in the known universe, human beings, right?

A simple sales project may involve a myriad of personalities, personal motivations, as well as analytical styles and requirements. It may involve people of different ages, beliefs, genders, and cultures. Decisions can be affected by personal ethics and group or company objectives. Throw in the variety of products and services to be sold, payment terms, and all the rest, and it's amazing that anything ever gets sold at all.

But obviously, things do get sold. From industrial cleaners, toothpicks, airplanes, shoes, household appliances, life insurance, and advertising, to just about anything you can think of, all these items are sold by professional salespeople who are performing their roles. And those professionals who have a strong mastery of sales basics are continually the top performers, regardless of industry, location, or sale process.

The Inside Game: Sales Basics covers a wide variety of topics including product knowledge and belief, effective targeting of prospects, understanding client needs, when to sell features and when to sell benefits, developing trust, how to make cold calls, when and how to give presentations, time management, lead generation, closing techniques and more.

These skills, and many others, are all important fundamental activities that aspiring star performers, and those already at the top of their game, need to master and continually review.

For those just getting started, this may seem like a daunting task. Don't worry. The good news is many of these skills, such as effective communication and developing trust, are things we've been doing our whole lives. We just need to understand how to brings these skills into the context of a sales environment in an effective and proper manner.

To get that understanding and to get started on the road to mastering the key fundamentals of sales, I would suggest that you that read this book in a staged manner, taking time to reflect how the content in each chapter relates to your current role. Please highlight and take note of items that are helpful to you and regularly review those sections.

When you have finished this book, create an action plan for the development of your sales skills and knowledge. Your plan should include which skills you want to improve and develop and the exact dates and times that you will be putting everything else aside to focus on your own development.

Most importantly, keep in mind that, due to the complexity of the sales, complete mastery is rarely attained. However, a common trait of star performers is that they practice continual learning. Every action and interaction can have an educational value if we look for it.

So, whenever you've completed a sales related activity, or interacted with a client or prospect, reflect back and mentally record what went well and what could have been improved. You'll discover that, often times, the application of simple sales fundamentals could have improved the outcome. You will also discover that the simple act of reflecting on your actions will greatly facilitate your professional development and improved sales performance.

In the end, no matter what you are selling or to whom you are selling, you will discover that if you focus on developing and ultimately mastering the fundamentals of your sales game, you will, without a doubt, become a top performer.

Happy Sales!

Mark Shriner

Knowledge and Belief

"A mediocre idea that generates enthusiasm will go further than a great idea that inspires no one." - Mary Kay Ash

Product knowledge and product belief are two of the most important components of your sales foundation. They are important because, unless you really know your product, it will be difficult for you believe in it. And if you don't believe in what you are selling, it will be difficult, if not impossible, for you to sell it.

Can you image how difficult it would be to sell something you didn't believe in? For example, if you knew that a particular product did not perform as promised, wouldn't you feel bad about trying to sell it to your prospects? Wouldn't you worry about complaints from dissatisfied customers? And wouldn't you lose respect for your company and fellow salespeople knowing that they were misleading their customers?

In fact, actions that aren't congruent with what we know to be the correct manner of acting cause cognitive dissonance, a sort of mental tug-of-war with opposing thoughts and emotions. This in turn can lead to lack of focus, poor performance, and even depression. And who needs that, right?

In order to completely align your thoughts and actions, you need to believe that whatever you are doing is the right thing to do. You need to believe that the product or service you are selling is the right thing to sell and will deliver on whatever you have promised.

Additionally, if you want to sell something effectively, your target audience should be able to see and feel your excitement and belief in your product. In order for this to occur, you yourself need to believe in and be excited about the product or service that you are selling. If you don't believe in what you are selling, it will loudly and clearly come across to your audience.

The fastest way to develop belief is to learn everything possible about the product or service that you are selling. Study it, use it, and compare it to the competition.

By doing this you will learn the strong points and how best to position your product or service. Even if you uncover some weak points, you will have a chance to understand why they exist, what are the potential ramifications for your client, and what possible alternatives there are.

If you don't do your homework and learn about your product, you will be reluctant to discuss it in detail, as you will fear being asked questions that you can't answer. You may also be worried that there might be issues with the product that you aren't aware of yet.

The best way to strip away that fear is to become the expert. Once you know your product inside out and know what are the ideal applications of that product, you will become perfectly comfortable introducing it to prospective clients. You won't be guessing. You will know, deep down, that in many situations your solution is the best for your clients and you will be able to explain why. At the same time, your prospective clients will appreciate the knowledge that you bring to the table and will respect you as a subject matter expert.

This is one of the reasons that life insurance companies spend so much time educating their sale force about the importance of life insurance. If their people don't really believe that life insurance is important, how can they convince others to buy it from them?

To that end, one of the first thing life insurance sales people are persuaded to do is to buy their own life insurance policies. By doing so, they learn about the process, the benefits, and satisfaction that comes from purchasing an important financial product.

Some of the most effective ways to develop product knowledge include studying all available marketing materials, white papers, and client testimonials. You can also create feature comparison charts for competitive products. You can do role-playing exercises with your colleagues where you try to sell competing products against your own.

One of my favorite ways to learn about a particular product or service is to shadow a successful sales person and watch how they introduce the service to prospective clients. Afterwards, I question the salesperson to find out what they believe are the product's strong points and weak points.

That said, there is no real shortcut for acquiring product knowledge. It takes time and effort to study and learn about the product and the competition. However, it is time well spent, as the knowledge you acquire will lead directly to product belief. This will result in greater enthusiasm for your work and ultimately, improved performance.

At the end of the day, if you are knowledgeable about your product and believe in it, you will be more confident in front of prospects and clients. You will enjoy your job more. And your confidence and enthusiasm will play a big part in convincing your prospective clients to buy from you.

So study, study, practice, practice, and good things will happen. That is something star performers both believe and do. You should too!

Development Activity

1. Make a list of all the positive and negative things about your company, your product, and your service.

2. If there are things that you are unsure of or cause you to doubt some aspect of what you selling, ask your sales manager or colleagues about this issue and how they deal with it.

Targeting

"Lack of direction, not lack of time, is the problem. We all have twenty-four hour days." - Zig Ziglar

Okay, so know you are an expert on the product or service you are selling, you believe in what you are selling, and you are ready to introduce it to the world. The problem is, as you will soon find out, that most of the world isn't interested in your product or service. In fact, it's usually, but not always, quite the opposite.

That being the case, smart targeting is crucial to your success. Smart targeting for business-to-business (B2B) sales means targeting organizations that are likely to have a need for your product or service, and contacting the appropriate people in those organizations.

For example, if you are selling international calling plans, you probably wouldn't want to contact companies that are only doing business domestically. Or, if you are selling copy machine services, you definitely wouldn't want to contact a manufacturer of copy machines. While these are very obvious examples, the point remains valid even for the less obvious.

Sometimes, even companies in a target industry or in a targeted geographic area can turn out to be inappropriate as prospects for your what you are selling. Maybe they are too small or too large for your product or service. Maybe they are restricted because of ownership structure, financial or legal difficulties, or perhaps they have been locked into a competitor's service for the next several years.

Please remember this! Every time you target an incorrect company or individual you waste your two most valuable assets, your time and your energy.

To avoid wasting time and effort by contacting inappropriate targets you should create a profile of the organizations that are most likely to be using a similar service or be in need of what you are selling. Your company can probably help you with this, as it might have already been created by more senior sales people in the organization and would typically be the focus of your company's marketing campaigns.

Items to consider can include:
Industry
Location
Size
Ownership Structure
Credit Rating
Number of Offices

Of course, a proven track record or an expected need of using products or services similar to the ones you are selling should be at the top of the list.

You should use these criteria and any others that your management team can provide you for selecting which organizations to contact. But your targeting efforts don't stop there.

If you are contacting the local office of a large organization with many offices, you will need to find out if the buying decision for what you are selling is made locally, at the headquarters, or jointly. If the decision isn't made locally, you will either have to follow up with HQ directly, or have the appropriate person in your company do so.

This will all take additional time and coordination, which is fine if you are able to land enough business to justify the effort. However, if your company's sales territory guidelines don't support or allow joint sales efforts, you may end up wasting your time. That is, if the decision maker isn't in your region, it may not make sense for you to reach out them.

Much of the initial targeting information can be uncovered by researching online or by filtering through prospect databases. However, there's also a fair amount of information that can only be discovered by communicating with prospects on the phone, via email, or in person. That's why it's important to have a list of qualifying questions that, once asked to the target, will help you quickly understand whether or not they are an appropriate target.

For the international calling services example, the question might be, "Can you tell me if your company provides services in any other countries?" Or, "Does your company do business overseas?" If the answer is yes, you would want to ask follow up questions to understand how much the company spends on international communications, what providers they are currently using, and who is responsible for choosing providers or evaluating competitive services.

By getting this information at the outset, you can hopefully avoid following up with a company that either doesn't need your services, or uses such a small quantity that it wouldn't be an attractive sales target for you.

Once you have identified an appropriate target, IE an organization that either uses or plans to use your product or service in the relatively near future, you get to the second part of targeting, which is finding the key people in the organization who are either the decision makers or who can influence the decision. If you fail to do this, you risk spending time talking to and meeting with people that don't have the ability to help your cause.

While target organizations can often be identified before contacting the organization, identifying key people usually requires some contact with the organization. That is, you will need to call, email, or have a conversation with someone who can tell you who is involved in the buying decisions for your type of service.

In some industries or for some services, you may be able to make an educated guess as to who the decision makers will be. For example, if you are selling an IT related product or service, the Chief Technology Officer (CTO) will often be involved. However, if the software facilitates marketing services, the key person may be the Chief Marketing Officer (CMO) and the CTO may just be an influencer.

Just as your company or colleagues can often provide you with a profile of target organizations, they may also be able to provide a profile of the target buyers in those companies. This can be very helpful, especially if you are able to search for individuals using databases and social networks such as LinkedIn.

When you reach out to the target person in a targeted organization, you will need to quickly identify whether they are in fact the key people, and if not, who is. This can be accomplished by asking the right questions.

Typical questions include:

"Can you tell me who is responsible for ordering these types of services?"

"Can you help me understand your company's process for buying this service?"

"Who would be the best person for me to follow up in order for me to introduce my product?"

20

Even when you have a name, it's always good to confirm before meeting with the person if they are, in fact, a decision maker. And during your meeting with that person, you shouldn't hesitate to ask whether or not other individuals are involved in the decision making process.

You could ask, for example, "Can you tell me if there are any other people involved in this decision?" Or, "I'd like to send some additional information. Is there anyone else I should send it to?"

With proper targeting of both organizations and individuals you will be spending your time in a more effective manner. Both you and the people you meet will feel that the time has been well spent. And, you will close more deals.

Development Activity

Create a target profile of both your target organizations and target buyers in those organizations.

Prospecting

"If we should be blessed by some great reward, such as fame or fortune, it's the fruit of a seed planted by us in the past." - Bodhidharma

Great salespeople are like good hunters. In fact, they are good hunters. That is, they know where to look for prospects and are very skilled in finding, making contact, and selling to them.

Once you have identified the types of organizations or individuals you want to target, you will need to know where and how to make contact with them. There are several ways to do this.

You may be able to get the information from your coworkers. If they have experience pursuing the same types of prospects, they may already know the best places.

If they don't, or if you want to come up with your own prospecting plan, you can consider looking in some of the following areas.

If you are targeting organizations or individuals in a specific industry, you should find all the relevant industry associations to see what databases, newsletters and events are available.

For example, if you are targeting companies in the oil recycling industry, there is a large industry association called NORA with hundreds of members. If you visit the NORA website at: http://www.noranews.org/, you can find a list of members, a list of upcoming events, advertising and sponsorship information, and other ways for you to make contact with NORA members.

Likewise, if you are targeting dentists in specific regions, say, Washington State for example, you could visit the Washington State Dental Association website at: http://www.wsda.org/, and find much of the same information.

Sometimes these associations will only provide basic member information to non-members. You may be able to get a list of members. But you may not be able to see the contact details, etc. In this situation, you can either look for the contact details yourself, or you may check with the association to see if you can purchase an annual directory or a database of members. You may even consider joining the association.

If you are not targeting a specific industry but a specific job function such marketing executives or Chief Financial Officers, you can find associations and events that cater to those fields as well. For example, The Association of Canadian Financial Officers, or the American Marketing Association would allow you to target those two fields.

You can also usually find print and online publications with targeted readership that matches the industry or demographic you are looking to target. For example, if you are looking to sell to IT professionals, you may want to look at CIO Magazine or Infoworld.

If you don't have an advertising budget, you may be able to rent the publication's readership database to conduct a mailing campaign. Or, you may be able to attend one of the events that they sponsor.

If you don't have a specific industry or field in mind, but instead are targeting a broader range of organizations or individuals, you may want join a local chamber of commerce or at least attend their events.

Having spent many years doing business outside of the U.S., I have found the American Chamber of Commerce in many countries around the world to be a great resource for information, networking, and developing new business opportunities. Inside the U.S. almost every city has some type of local business chamber of commerce.

Additionally, joining service organizations such as Rotary and the Lions may help you to meet more people. Typically these organizations don't encourage active solicitation of business and also expect that members contribute to the organization by serving on committees assisting with events.

There are networking groups and organizations such as BNI (www.bni.com) that do encourage members to do business and even require members to make introductions and referrals to each other.

Social media sites such as LinkedIn can be very helpful. You can use the advanced search function to search for people and filter by company name, location, and job title. If you aren't getting enough results when you search, you may want to consider signing up for one of the paid memberships which provide access to a larger network, more information about that network, and extra options for communicating directly with people in that network.

For example, if you'd like meet people in the marketing department of Microsoft in Redmond, Washington, you can search for:

Company name: Microsoft

Keyword: marketing

Location: Redmond.

Once you see the results, you will have different options to make contact with individuals shown.

Sometimes the first step is to invite the person to connect. However, many people will refuse requests to connect from people that haven't met in person. So, when possible, you should send a short note explaining the reason you'd like to connect along with your invitation.

For example, "Dear Susan, I'd like to share some important industry research regarding marketing for IT companies. Please connect and I will then forward the information to you." Or, "Dear Susan, I have a business opportunity related to IT marketing I'd like to discuss with you. Please connect and I will send you more information."

If the person still doesn't accept your invitation to connect, you may just try to email them directly as some people do display their email addresses on their LinkedIn profile page. Or you might just call the main telephone number of the company and ask to speak to that person.

Another alternative is to call the company and explain that you'd like to email some information to the person and ask for the email address. Usually, the main telephone receptionist will not give out this information. However, if you can get a hold of the person's assistant and explain the reason you are calling, often times they will give you the email address.

Lastly, if you have mutual connections or are separated by only few people, you might want to ask the people in your network to make an introduction on your behalf.

Another important source of prospecting is your existing network of friends, family, colleagues, clients and prospects. Don't be afraid to ask people for introductions to new prospects. I have found that satisfied clients can be among the best referral sources as they can testify to the quality of work you do and often times are eager for you to grow your business.

In this case, the best time to ask for a referral is just after you have delivered value to the client and they have acknowledged it. At this time, you could say something along the lines of "John, I'm glad to hear that you are happy with our service. We have enjoyed working with you on this project and look forward to the next one. Would you happen to know anyone else in your organization that might benefit from our services?"

Many professional service providers will send thank you notes or information updates to their clients, and sometimes conclude with a message such as, "One of the greatest compliments I can receive is a referral or introduction from a satisfied client."

The point is to keep in touch with your network frequently enough so that when someone has an opportunity to make an introduction, your name will be at the top of their mind.

Just as prospectors mine for gold, sales prospecting is where you will find your future gold. It is the activity that builds the foundation of your sales pipeline and is the single most important activity for sales people. If you are a good prospector, you will be a good sales person.

Development Activity

1. Create a written description of your ideal prospect.
2. List three different methods or locations for you to locate your ideal prospects.
3. Establish a weekly goal for prospecting activity, either in terms of time spent or number of prospects identified.

Get the Meeting!

"If a picture is worth a thousand words, a face-to-face meeting is easily worth a thousand pictures." – Mark Shriner

Face-to-face meetings provide a great opportunity to meet new people, learn, develop trust, share knowledge, and improve your communication and sales skills.

If your sales process involves any type of face-to-face client contact, then getting the meeting with a qualified prospect should be one of your top priorities. Not only will getting the meeting bring you one giant step closer to closing a deal, it will also help you in many other areas of your work and professional development.

If you can't get a meeting with a prospect, you run the risk of not being taken seriously, or simply overlooked. Everyone that we sell to today is continually bombarded with offers, invites, emails, and phone calls. If you are just another contributor to the "noise" that your prospects have to deal with, it will be very difficult for you to differentiate yourself from the competition or even get the attention of your prospect.

Social Media; No Substitute for Meetings

Making connections on LinkedIn or other social media sites can be helpful but should never be considered a substitute for face-to-face meetings. Sure it's easy to do, and sometimes will even pay off by allowing you to get in touch with a legitimate prospect.

However, it IS NOT a substitute for real client and prospect meetings. Don't fall into the trap of convincing yourself that since you have a lot of connections on LinkedIn or on some other social media site, you are somehow making progress and are on track to be a top performer.

As previously stated, getting a face-to-face meeting allows you to develop rapport with your prospect and get an understanding of their needs as well as your opportunities and challenges. It can also be the start of a new business relationship and an opportunity for you to cultivate the trust of your client.

Lastly, and by no means least, meeting with prospects and clients gives you a chance to develop your communication skills, increase your market and product knowledge, and add to your professional network.

Since experts in human communication commonly state that most communication between humans is non-verbal, how can we expect to develop effective and meaningful communications with our prospects if we don't meet them in person?

That is not to say that we cannot communicate via email, phone or videoconferences. It's just that it's usually a lot easier and faster to have open, honest, and meaningful communications in person or after we have met someone in person at least once.

Let's first talk about how to get the meeting. And then, in later chapters, we will discuss how to prepare, plan for, and conduct a meeting in an effective manner.

To start with, most prospects will typically try to avoid committing to a face-to-face meeting as they, like all of us, are challenged by not having enough time in the day to get their regular tasks finished. As such, most people are very protective of their calendars and covet any open spots that they might have.

In order to have your meeting requests accepted, you will first need to make your requests as attractive to your prospects as possible. You can do this by making sure your prospect sees the benefit for them to meet with you. They will all be evaluating your request by asking themselves a simple question, "What's in it for me?"

Things your prospect might be looking for include information about new trends in the industry, news about the competition, or information about new technologies or products that is relevant or helpful to the work that they do.

Other incentives to meet include a chance for your prospect to be introduced to someone in an influential position or an opportunity to meet with industry peers. This can be done by hosting a small round table discussion or by inviting an industry expert to participate in a meeting.

Sometimes incentives might not even be linked to work. It might a chance to participate in an activity that your prospect enjoys such as golf, or a charity auction, etc. Sometimes it could be something as simple as grabbing a cup of coffee, lunch, dinner, or an after work drink.

Whatever hook you are going to use to help you get the meeting, you need to introduce it in a clear and concise manner either on the phone or via email.

If it is your first contact, you should start with stating who you are, what you do, what you want, and the benefit that you'd like to bring to the table for your prospect.

For example, during an initial phone call you might say something like this, "Hi. This is Mark Shriner from The Inside Game. We work with the leading companies in your industry to help them cut costs and optimize their manufacturing operations. I'd like to stop by, introduce myself, and share some research regarding the latest industry trends in factory automation related to cost cutting. Are you available next Tuesday or Wednesday afternoon?"

You can see that the first sentence introduces myself then my company. The second sentence explains what my company does and our relevance to the prospect. It also gives my company and me some credibility (i.e "we work with the leading companies in your industry..."). The third sentence states what I want and also what is the benefit for my prospect.

In actual practice, I typically would ask a couple of questions just after my intro to build some rapport and also learn more about the prospect's current practices and needs. For example, I might ask, "Have you ever worked with an outside consultant to do an operational audit?" Or, "Can you tell me a little bit about how your company measures operational efficiency?"

If the prospect openly responds, you should try to keep the conversation going to learn more about their needs. You don't want to talk too much about what you do or give too much information about your company or offering. If you do, you may find that the prospect feels that they have enough information about you and don't need to meet in person.

When communicating via email, you can't really ask many questions and there is much less interactivity. However, you can use email to provide more background information and introduce more potential benefits that you can deliver if the prospect is willing to meet.

Again though, you should avoid sending too much information. For starters, most of it probably won't get read. Secondly, you run the risk of not getting the meeting as the prospect will feel that they have all the information they need.

Regardless of how well you make your pitch, often times your initial meeting requests will be denied or deflected. It's nothing to worry about. It's simply an opportunity to further develop your sales and communication skills by first listening to the reason for declining the meeting and then responding in an effective manner.

Common responses to meeting requests include:

"Can you just email me some more information?"

"Send me a link to your website and I'll get back to you if I have any questions."

"Let me check with my colleagues to see if there is a need."

"We aren't currently looking for a new provider."

Don't let these responses deter you. You can and should still try to persuade your prospect that there will be some benefit in meeting with you. You may want to counter the above type of meeting refusals with responses such as:

"I would love to send you some information. The problem is that until I have a better understanding of your current situation and needs, I'm really not sure what would be the most appropriate *information to send you. To that end, would you be open to just a short meeting, or, if not, letting me ask you a few more questions about your current situation?"*

"I'll send you a link. But please keep in mind that much of the information that would be most valuable to you isn't currently available on our site. Would it be alright for me to stop by for few minutes to say hi, introduce myself, and provide you with some of our latest research?"

"While you are checking with your colleagues, would it be ok if I dropped by to say hello and give you some of the latest research on trends in our industry?"

"I understand that you aren't in the market for a new provider. And I'm not going to try to sell anything to you. I'd simply like to say hello and give you an overview of the technology and processes that we have developed for a few of your major competitors including (company name). Then, going forward, if you ever need more information or would like to get a second opinion about your current processes, you would always be welcome to contact us."

Please don't feel the need to use these responses word for word. Craft your own replies that are appropriate to your situation and your prospect's needs, and are in line with your communication style.

The basic formula of acknowledging the person's request or objection, and then countering with both an appeal to being friendly ("stop by and say hello"), and adding an additional benefit ("provide you with some of our latest research") has, time and time again, proven to be an effective way to getting an initial meeting.

If these approaches are not successful, you can always agree to send your prospect the information or materials that they have requested and, at the same time, ask their permission to follow up with them in a few weeks to confirm receipt of the information and to see if they have any questions.

Most people will agree to this and it can work to your favor. The prompt delivery of information and the timely follow up will allow you to demonstrate that you are dependable and can be trusted to follow up on commitments.

If approaches like this on the phone aren't effective, you may want to try inviting your prospect to an activity that they might feel is more beneficial or enjoyable for them. For example, a round-table discussion with peers in their industry or a networking event.

Alternatively, you may simply invite them to an entertainment activity such as a golf outing, a cocktail reception, or even a business lunch or dinner.

Whatever approach you take, don't lose sight of your target, which is to get the meeting. That is the point where the sales process and your professional development really start to take off.

Another benefit of meeting with prospects and clients is that the more meetings you have, the more opportunities you will get to practice your presentation and communication skills. This will lead to greater confidence which will snowball into better results. And since you are having so many meetings, your sales pipeline will rapidly expand which is a key for both success and confidence.

In short, if you are booked solid for meetings, you will feel a lot more confident about your skills and your chances of success.

For example, if you only have one meeting scheduled for the week, you will feel a lot of pressure to get a positive outcome from that single meeting. You may even feel a little desperate and try to force the sale. That's a recipe for disaster as your prospects may pick up on your desperation, and you will definitely not be enjoying the meeting.

However, if you have several meetings scheduled during the week, you won't worry so much about the outcome of any single meeting. You will be more relaxed and your prospects will be more open to you.

In conclusion, getting a meeting with a prospective client is one of the most important objectives for professional sales people. In fact, you can often judge a person's sales ability solely on the number of meetings that they regularly attend. So, get out there and get those meetings!

Development Activity

Find out the standard number of meetings that your colleagues have each week and establish a target of your own.

Directing the Meeting

"Only you can control your future." – Dr. Seuss

OKAY, so you get the meeting, now what? Now the fun starts! The meeting is your show and it's up to you to be both the director and the co-star.

What do I mean by that? Well for starters, anytime you get one or more human beings together in the same room, unexpected, random things can happen. But you aren't meeting with your prospects to observe and verify the randomness of the universe or of human nature.

You are meeting with your prospects because you want to develop a business relationship, learn about their needs, begin to develop trust, and ultimately, sell something to them.

Ultimately, you should strive to achieve something at the meeting that will get you at least one step closer to closing a deal and generating revenues.

Therefore, it is critical that you have a game plan for each meeting that includes a clear understanding of what exactly you'd like to get out of the meeting, and how you're going to get it. In that sense you are the director of the meeting. If we wanted to take the analogy further, I guess we could say that you are also the writer of the script as well.

All too often salespeople consider the meeting the final target. But we should never go to meetings just for the sake of having a meeting or getting acquainted with our prospects. This approach often results in having meetings with people who really aren't our target, or having meetings that don't really achieve anything other than taking up our valuable time. Remember, every meeting should move you closer to your ultimate goal, the sale.

What are some legitimate targets for prospect meetings? For starters, we can attempt to close a deal. This is more likely to happen if you are selling lower cost goods or services and when the client has an immediate need. For example, if you are leasing copier machines and a new business owner has decided that they need a professional grade copy machine in the office, you may have a good shot at closing the deal on the first meeting.

If you are selling low cost stationery or corporate gifts, you might be able to sell some of your products right from the start.

For many products and services, closing a deal at the first meeting might not be a realistic goal. Instead, you may want to shoot for targets such as getting anyone of the following from your prospect:

A request for a proposal from you
A request for additional information from you
An agreement to test your services
An agreement from the prospect to arrange a meeting between you and other stakeholders in your prospect's company
Getting a referral to another prospect.

What is Your Objective?

Before going into meetings with salespeople that I work with or coach, I almost always ask the question, "What is our objective?" I have found that how the person responds is one of the most important indicators of their success in sales.

If they don't know or are unsure of their objective, or if they name something like "to meet the prospect," or "to introduce our company," they typically aren't a top performer.

However, if they respond with an objective that will get them at one least step closer to the sale, and they have a plan in place on how to direct the meeting towards that end, they are, or soon will be, a star performer.

Two secondary objectives that should constantly run in parallel with your primary meeting goals include gaining an understanding of your prospect's needs, concerns, and buying processes, and finding a way to incrementally increase the amount of trust that your prospect has in you.

These goals are both very important components of your success. However, since achieving them doesn't actually move you closer to a deal, we count them as secondary, or supplementary, goals.

The most effective way to increase the likelihood of achieving both your primary and your secondary goals is to first clearly decide on how you will move the sales process forward (i.e. an agreement to entertain a proposal, trial of service, etc.), and then to set the agenda and manage the meeting flow accordingly.

In short, you should have a clear plan on how you can steer the meeting towards your desired outcome. This can best be done at the beginning of the meeting.

Typically, an initial meeting will start with a little rapport building or small talk about your trip to the office, the weather, sports, or some other light conversation. Once you and your prospect have broken the ice, you can kick off the real business by suggesting a flow for the meeting.

For example, you can say something like this, "I appreciate you taking the time to meet me today. Before I introduce our company and the solutions that we provide, would you mind giving me an introduction to your team and the processes you are currently using?"

When I do this, I ensure that I am able to get some initial information about the prospect. This will help me to better frame or filter the information that I will later provide regarding my company and our products or services.

In short, I have a chance to learn what is relevant and important to my prospect. Setting up the meeting flow also helps me to avoid the meeting going off track.

Earlier I stated that, in addition to being the director, you should also the role of co-star. Why the co-star and not the star?

In the great majority of all meetings, it's much better to have your prospect do more of the talking than you. When your prospect is talking, they are sharing information with you about their company, their needs, their buying process, the challenges that you will be facing, and often times, important information about themselves. All of this information is valuable and will help your cause.

However, if you monopolize the meeting by taking the starring role for yourself, it will be very difficult for you to get any of the above information or learn about your prospect. Furthermore, you will miss out on a great opportunity to connect with your prospect on a personal level.

Most of us, after a certain level of comfort is attained, prefer talking than listening. In most cases, our favorite topics happen to be ourselves, our jobs, our families, our challenges, and our plans.

This is true in business situations as well. We are all faced with challenges in the office, and talking about these challenges is something that most people find to be both comforting and beneficial, as we are able to get feedback and hopefully some good ideas on how to better manage.

I've found that in many cases when a prospect or client takes the time to share a great deal of information about their personal situation (when selling to individuals) or their company's situation (when selling to businesses), not only do I develop a stronger connection with them, but they also become reluctant to begin the buying process again with a potential competitor. That is, once they have invested their time and energy to spell out their needs to me, they are, at one level, personally invested in our working relationship and my success.

The more time a client spends talking about their needs and sharing information with me, the stronger this connection becomes. The opposite is also true. If I spend all the time talking, the client will probably only retain a portion of what I say, but they will feel that I'm more concerned with selling than listening. An opportunity to develop trust and establish a business relationship will have been lost.

Therefore, it is imperative that we, as sales people, spend more time listening than talking, especially during the first meeting.

A good rule of thumb for me is that during a one-hour meeting, the prospect should be talking for at least 30-40 minutes of the time. The ratio may change depending on what you're selling, the number people in attendance, and the personalities involved. However, regardless of these factors, you should have a good strategy for getting your prospects to open up and share information with you during your meetings.

Okay, so now you have built up some rapport, set the meeting flow, and learned from your prospect about their current situation and needs. What's next? Don't forget what you came for! In fact, everything so far should have been leading the meeting towards that objective.

If your goal was to get your prospect to agree to receive a proposal, you will need to put that offer on the table. How you do it will often times affect the likelihood of acceptance.

For example, if you simply say, "Can I send you a proposal?" your prospect may feel that you haven't fully understood their needs, and they may not even be clear on what you will be proposing. They definitely won't be eagerly awaiting your proposal.

However, if you were to say, "Just to be sure that I clearly understand the information you've shared, would it be alright for me to summarize what we have discussed?" You would then summarize the main points that the prospect has shared with you and ask them, "Have I accurately summarized what've you told me?"

This not only shows that you have sincerely listened to your prospect, thus developing trust, but it also gives your prospect a chance to modify or add any important details.

You then propose the next step. For example, "Based upon what you have shared with me, I believe we could bring some significant value to the table both in terms of reducing your current costs and also in terms of improving the efficiency of your operations. With that in mind, would you be open to receiving a proposal for these services?"

Most of the time, the response will be positive. Thus, you will have accomplished your primary objective of moving closer to the sale. If you asked intelligent questions and were an empathetic listener during the meeting, you probably also accomplished your supplementary goals of learning about your prospect and establishing a foundation of trust.

This same pattern of managing the meeting flow, gathering information, summarizing the contents of the meeting, and suggesting a next step will almost always get you one or more steps closer to the sale. But remember, it's up to you, the director and co-star, to make it happen. And the first and most important step to doing so is having a clearly defined plan before the meeting starts.

Meeting Preparation

Another important, but often overlooked factor in conducting a successful meeting with a client or prospect is doing a little research about the company and people you will be meeting.

If you show up and demonstrate that you understand the company's business and know about some of the recent projects or events the company has been involved in, you will come across as being professional.

However, if you come to the meeting and ask very basic questions and make it obvious that you have no idea what your prospect's company or industry is about, it will be difficult for you to gain their trust and their business.

So please take a few minutes to visit their website, search for recent headlines and press releases related to the company. If you haven't already, you may want to look at your prospect's profile on LinkedIn to see what other jobs they have held, what companies they have worked for, what professional organizations they belong to, and even where they went to school. All of this info can be useful to you, and if used at the right time can help you to get closer to your prospect and closer to the sale.

Development Activity

1. Before each meeting clearly state your objectives and your plan for achieving them.

2. Create a short list of key data that you should know about any prospect before meeting them.

Effective Presentations

"There are always three speeches for everyone you actually gave. The one you practiced, the one you have gave, and the one you wish you gave." – Dale Carnegie

"It usually takes me more than three weeks to prepare a good impromptu speech." – Mark Twain

Even though I'm a big believer in the effectiveness of interactive sales discussions whereby we use the time with our prospects to get them to open up and teach us about their business needs, there are times when giving a presentation is required. When this is the case, it is very important to properly plan what and how you will present.

Using boilerplate presentations that are simply recycled from one meeting to the next is not an effective way to engage with prospects. In fact, you may even find that this approach positions you and your company in a negative light.

If you treat your prospects like they are all the same and don't have any unique qualities, it's highly likely that your prospects will sense this. Thus, in their eyes, you will be the same as most other sales people who show up and push their own agenda without considering their prospects' needs.

Please do take the time to plan your presentation and to customize the material that you will be presenting.

To best do this, you will need to understand a few things. What's the purpose of your presentation? Is it to build trust, establish credibility, or educate your customer? Or is it to offer a solution or try to close deal? Your purpose could be any number of things. However, if you don't consciously take it into consideration, you may end up presenting the wrong information or presenting in the wrong way.

Other factors that you should take into consideration when planning your presentation include:

Who will be attending the presentation?

How will they be judging you and your company?

Who is your competition?

What are the key factors in your client's buying decision?

You will want to present information that will make your prospect want to do business with you. This includes establishing your credibility and demonstrating your expertise in your industry. It also includes presenting in a friendly manner that makes you likeable to your prospect.

You should also consider how you will differentiate your offering from that of your competitors. Lastly, and maybe most importantly, you should think about how can achieve all of the above in a memorable manner that will allow your audience to remember the key points of your presentation.

Presentation Checklist

1. What is the purpose of the presentation?

2. Who will be attending the presentation and how will they be judging you and your company?

3. What are the key factors in your audience's buying decision?

4. Who are the competition and what are their strengths and weaknesses?

5. How can I differentiate myself from the competition?

6. How can I make the key points of my presentation memorable?

You start off with identifying the purpose of the presentation, because that, more than anything, will affect what and how you should present. There are at least two purposes or reasons for every presentation: the stated reason, which you share with your client, and the unstated reason which is our real focus.

Stated reasons for presentations can include introducing your company, presenting a specific proposal, introducing a new technology, process, or solution, and sharing relevant industry research.

While the stated reason for the presentations may vary and should help to shape the presentation, the unstated reason is always to get you closer, if not all the way, to a buying decision. As that is the case, ask yourself how your presentation will accomplish this.

Will it conclude with a call for action? Will it convince your prospect to share additional information with you? Will it gain your prospect's commitment to move to the next step in the buying process? Be very specific in your approach to how any of these targets will be accomplished or facilitated by your presentation.

You will want to know who will be attending the presentation and how they will be judging you. For example, if the CFO is attending, he or she will most likely be interested in costs or on the effects on the bottom line. Or, they may be interested in potential tax benefits.

However, representatives from the sales team will probably be more interested in how you can help them to be more competitive in the market or help them to generate more sales leads, etc. Likewise, someone from the HR department might be interested in knowing whether your service will increase or decrease their workload or deliver some benefit to their team.

You should always try to get the attendee list in advance. You may even want to contact the attendees in advance to introduce yourself and ask them if there is a particular area of interest for them.

For example, you could send an email that asks, "In order to make sure that I present the information that is most helpful to you, would you mind sharing with me any key questions or concerns that you'd like me to address?"

If it's not practical to contact each attendee individually, you might want to work with one of your contacts in the company to ask them about the attendees and learn about their concerns. You could also inquire about group dynamics and try to understand who will be main drivers of any potential business.

If you are in a competitive situation, or you are trying to displace a competitor, you should get a clear understanding of your competitor's strengths and weaknesses. You should then decide how best to address these with your presentation.

For example, you may want to avoid speaking negatively about the competition or even mentioning the competition by name. One way to do this is to present findings from third-party industry experts or research organizations that show your product or service in a positive light when compared to your competitors.

Another way is to create a buyer's checklist that can be used by your prospect to evaluate competing companies, products and services. By doing this, you may be able to frame or determine some of the evaluation processes used by your prospect.

And by pre-filling out the form with all of the key information about your company and product or service, you are making it easier for your prospect to see all the key features of your offering in one simple document.

"No one can remember more than three points."

– Philip Crosby

Making key points of a presentation memorable can be challenging. You are competing for mindshare, not just with your competitors, but with everything else that's going on in the days and lives of the people in attendance.

People are incredibly busy and constantly barraged with massive amounts of information from phone calls, emails, and meetings. The need to multitask is a constant. I've witnessed presentations where all the attendees had their laptops open and were responding to emails during the whole time the presenter was speaking. Instead of feeling like he had center stage, the speaker started to feel like he was an intrusion to his audience.

In situations like this, how can you make sure your audience not only pays attention to what you are saying but is also able to retain the key points? As in all other aspects of sales, you need to have a plan and process.

For starters, do you yourself know what are the key points of your presentation? If you present all slides as equal and don't emphasize the content of one or two, you are setting yourself up to fail. Firstly and most importantly, you must decide what are the 2-3 main points that you want emphasize and that you want your audience to understand and remember.

Once you have decided on the key points, you need to build your presentation around them. This means that you structure the presentation in a manner that introduces the key points and continually refers to and reinforces them.

There are many ways to do this. For example you can follow the old standard method of telling your audience what you are going to present, present the content, then summarize what you have presented. This is sometimes explained as:

1. Tell them what you are going tell them.

2. Tell them.

3. Tell them what you told them.

Another similar approach is starting your presentation with something like the following:

"I'm going to be presenting a lot of information that should be useful to everyone here. However, there are really three main points that I'd like to make:

1. Our solution can help you dramatically reduce costs.

2. Our solution can be implemented in a very simple manner.

3. The ROI will be impressive and will happen in a very short time."

By starting your presentation in this manner, you've planted the seeds of your key messages. Now you simply have to support them with the information you present and then reinforce them with your conclusion.

Oftentimes salespeople feel that they should introduce their company's history, number staff, number and locations of offices, etc. I guess this is their way of trying to demonstrate that they are from an established and credible company.

I believe that spending too much time on this type of information at the outset of a presentation does nothing more than cause your audience's minds to start wandering on to other and perhaps more important things in their lives.

Nobody gets excited about your company's history or statistics. But they do get excited about things that can help them with their jobs or in their lives. That is where your focus should be.

If you desperately feel the need to spend some time introducing your company, you can simply prepare a few slides or a handout and say, "I've prepared some background information about our company. It's included in the handouts. If you'd like any additional information, please let me know."

When you do get to the slides that support the 2-3 points that you want to focus on, make sure you spend the appropriate amount of time on them. When you have made your point, ask your audience to confirm that you have made your point.

For example, "Would you all agree that this approach would help you to reduce your costs?"

By doing this you are encouraging your audience to participate in your presentation. This is important because the more you involve your audience, the greater the likelihood that they will focus on your message and remember the key points of your message.

Asking them to confirm the point you have made can also be an important step to remembering what you have said and towards getting your audience to accept your overall message.

After you have made a point and asked for confirmation, you can always refer back to the point. For example, "Okay, I've shown you how we can use this solution to reduce costs. Now I'll talk a little bit about how easy it is to implement."

Then, after you've presented the information about the ease of implementation and asked for confirmation of your point, you can repeat the process again. For example, "We've seen how this solution can dramatically reduce cost and how easy it is to implement, the last point we will discuss is the impressive ROI that can be expected."

When you get to the end your presentation, you can simply summarize your three points. Alternatively, you could ask your audience whether or not you were effective in communicating those points. Or, you may even want to ask your audience if they can name the three key points of your presentation.

Whatever your method, it's important that you clearly and concisely make your points, and continually reinforce them.

Another effective way to get your audience to remember the key points of your presentation is to tell a story that reinforces those points. Stories are oftentimes much more memorable than simple data points on a presentation slide.

You could tell a story of how another company benefited from the solution you are introducing. Or, you could tell a story of how your solution was developed to solve a particular problem or need. The key thing is using as many techniques as possible to keep your audience engaged and to help them remember the key points.

Personally, I prefer a more a casual or friendly style when presenting. I find that it makes it easier for me to interact with my audience. A formal approach can sometimes create an artificial wall between the presenter and their audience.

That being said, having worked for a couple of European companies, I can say that sometimes a formal approach is more appropriate. That's why it's really important to know your audience and also understand what style you are most comfortable with.

Another thing to consider is what materials you will use to make and support your presentation. Will you provide handouts? Will you present using a laptop or will you use an LCD projector?

Regardless of how you supply your support materials, printed, on a computer screen, or projected onto a larger wall or screen, you will want to make sure that the materials are effective at supporting and reinforcing your spoken message.

The materials shouldn't be the focus of the audience's attention. You should be. With that in mind, don't try to cram too many slides into your presentation, and definitely don't try to cram too much information on to each slide.

Creating slides that are chock full of text is a recipe for losing your audience's attention and putting them to sleep. This is especially true if, in an effort to include more text, you use a small font that makes it difficult for your audience to read.

Whatever font size you use, do not use more than three different sized fonts on a single slide. Doing so makes the slides seem messy and unorganized. More importantly, you should work to clearly present the key points in an easy to read manner that flows along with your presentation.

One of the biggest mistakes presenters can make is to simply read the text of their presentation. Again, this focuses the audience's attention onto the presentation materials, which can serve to make the speaker irrelevant.

I've seen speakers use handouts and then, as they start reading the information on the handouts word for word, they totally lose their audience. A clear sign this is happening is when the people in the audience start flipping through their handouts, reading ahead, and basically, not paying attention to what the speaker is saying.

To avoid scenarios like this, have something to say about each slide. For example, for a slide that shows the locations of your offices around the world, you wouldn't want to simply read of each location. Your audience can do that for themselves.

Instead, you can point out the benefit of this information to your audience. For example, you could say, "As you can see we have 20 offices in 15 countries. This allows us to provide 24-hour support to our clients regardless of where they are located."

Another use for slides or handouts is to provide a diagram or graphic that explains or supports what you are communicating. If you have described a custom workflow or process, you could display a detailed diagram to make it more clear to your audience.

Likewise, you could use a graph or chart to support your message about a particular trend, market condition, etc. The main thing to remember is that you and your message should be the focus, not the support materials. They are there simply to support you and make your message more clear and memorable to your audience.

At the end, that should be your aim. You want people to be engaged, to ask questions, to remember you and what you've said. If you do this, you will gain credibility in the eyes of your audience, and you will get one step closer to closing the deal.

Development Activity

1. What are the 2-3 most important things you would like to impress upon your audience during your standard presentations?

2. What techniques will you use to make it easier for your audience to remember those key points? How will you confirm whether or not they have understood and remembered them?

Features vs. Benefits

"People don't want to buy a quarter-inch drill, they want a quarter-inch hole." – Theodore Levitt

What are features? What are benefits? When should we talk about features? When should we talk about benefits? This chapter will answer these questions and go on to explain how best to introduce both.

There is a commonly accepted saying that successful sales people should "sell the sizzle, not the steak." In short, this is stating that salespeople should focus on the benefits of the product or service they are selling, not the features.

Using steak as an example, it's argued that it would be better to say, "This free range organic steak not only tastes great, but is a healthier choice," than simply saying, "This is an 8-ounce free range organic steak."

That is, the benefits of being healthy and tasting great are more exciting than the feature of being free range or organic.

Now, while most people would agree that the first description has a bit more sizzle and would probably sell more steaks, I'm going to make the argument that both features and benefits, i.e. the steak and the sizzle, are important, and it's up to you decide how and when to introduce them into your sales discussions.

The reason for this is that different buyers have different needs, different motivations, and different ways of analyzing their potential purchases. The purchaser of a photocopier machine might have very specific performance requirements for speed, color options, etc. In such cases, you will definitely need to talk about these features. However, you may also talk about some of the additional benefits associated with your product or company.

For example, if you uncover the fact that your prospect has fixed requirements for performance, pricing, size, etc., you can point out the features of your machine that address those requirements and also introduce some of the related benefits.

You could state, "Our machine not only meets your performance and budgetary requirements but will also be able to give you additional savings due to the super efficient use of toner, and the maintenance-free operation guarantee we provide. Furthermore, we have a financing plan that reduces the impact on your budget and provides certain tax benefits."

Now, I'm throwing a lot of benefits on that one example to demonstrate a point. In practice, you may want to tone it down a bit and simply introduce one or two benefits related to each feature.

When presenting product or company information, I always try to tie each feature to a specific benefit for the client.

For example, I might say, "You can see that we have offices in Asia, Europe and North America. This allows us to serve as a one-stop-provider for all your translation requirements. Not only can we cover over all major languages, we can provide 24-hour service to our clients by passing projects from one region to the next to be managed and returned the next day."

In this case the feature of having offices on three continents is tied to the benefit of being able to provide 24-hour service and to serve as a single provider for all of our client's translation needs.

Examples of Features and Benefits

Feature	Benefit
Compact	Used in small offices, Easy to lift
HDTV	Viewing quality, More detail
100 pages per minute	Reduce printing time by half, increased productivity of staff
400 Horsepower	Excellent acceleration, Capable of pulling large trailers
Offices in 60 countries	Easy to receive service
Airbags	Safety
Dual processor	Faster, More computing power
FDA Approved	Safe
Organic	Healthy, Environmentally safe

Again, sticking with the translation service provider example, I could state an offered feature as follows, "Our company uses Translation Memory." Or, I could make the benefit very clear to my prospect by saying something like, "We use Translation Memory, which helps to reduce costs and improve consistency."

Why do this? Believe it or not, a lot of the benefits that we, as salespeople find to be self evident, aren't self evident to our clients and prospects. They will rarely be as knowledgeable as we are about the products and services that we are selling. Sometimes, we find that much of what we say and do is fairly routine, so we forget that many of the features we are introducing might not be fully understood by our prospects.

Remember to slow down! Make sure your prospects and customers understand what you are talking about and fully comprehend the potential benefits to them. Of course, you don't want to seem like you are condescending or talking down to your audience. You just need to make sure that they get what you are saying and understand the related benefits.

One of the best ways to do this is to give examples or tell a story that clearly demonstrates the value or benefit of the product, service, or feature you are talking about. Not only are examples and stories more easily understood, they are also easier for most people to remember.

I once told a prospect a story about how our company had used a tool called Translation Memory to help a client reduce their translation costs by more than 50 percent. He later arranged several meetings with his colleagues so I could introduce our service. And every time I started to talk about Translation Memory, he would jump in and energetically tell the story for me.

It was very clear that he was excited about the benefits of Translation Memory and wanted to share the information with his colleagues. The story made it easy for him to do so.

With that in mind, I highly recommend that you prepare some relevant examples or stories to illustrate the features and benefits of your product or service. If you can't think of any, just ask your colleagues what examples or stories they use.

In conclusion, knowing the difference between features and benefits and how to present them is important. But, equally important is knowing when it is appropriate to introduce one or the other to your prospect. This takes practice, an understanding of your prospect's evaluation process, and the ability to clearly introduce your product's key features and their corresponding benefits.

Development Activity

Make a list of the key features of the product or service you are selling. When you are done, try to write down at least two benefits of each feature. Keep that list and review it from time to so that it becomes a natural part of the way you talk about what you are selling.

What's your USP?

"I believe that every guitar player inherently has something unique about their playing. They just have to identify what makes them different and develop it." – Jimmy Page

One of the most common questions asked by potential customers and clients is, "What makes you different from your competitors," or "How is your company better than the others?"

This is a fair question, and one that you should be adept at answering. It will allow you to differentiate yourself from the competition and demonstrate exactly why your prospect should meet and consider doing business with you.

What these people are really asking is, "What's your unique selling proposition?" A unique selling proposition, or USP for short, is the thing that differentiates your product, service, or company from the others. It's your competitive strength and the reason that many of your customers choose to do business with you.

Some famous examples of USPs include the following:

Domino's Pizza
You get fresh, hot pizza delivered to your door in 30 minutes or less or it's free

M&Ms
The milk chocolate melts in your mouth, not in your hand.

Evernote
Remember everything. Capture anything. Access anywhere. Find things fast. It's free.

Wal-Mart
We Sell For Less

Technically speaking, these examples are a cross between corporate taglines and USP statements. Often times, the USP is more complex than a simple tagline or a brief statement and might take some explaining.

An example would be a budget airline that provides free FM radio service to all passengers which none of the competitors offer. Another USP could be a paint company that sells paint in unique easy-to-open, easy-to-pour, and easy-to-store paint cans.

These USPs might not be spelled out in their respective company's advertisement buzz lines. But they are part of the larger marketing and sales message. They are what make these companies different from the rest.

But let's get back to your company and your service. Can you clearly and succinctly identify your USP? If so, do you believe it? Can you explain why it is true?

To be able to do this is incredibly important for your own product knowledge and belief and for you to be able to convince your prospects that there will be a benefit in talking or meeting with you.

Whatever your company's or your personal USP is, I encourage you to practice stating in a clear, easy to understand and appropriate manner. Make it sound natural and do NOT try to oversell it.

For example, if you were say, "We leverage industry-leading technology to create synergies between business stakeholders and maximize the ROI enterprise-wide," to someone you just met in an elevator, they might get the impression that you were just repeating something you'd read off your company's website or brochure.

Equally as bad, the person you are speaking with will probably not understand exactly what it is you are selling and may even be intimidated. Most people don't like to admit that they don't understand another person's elevator pitch, and are thus reluctant to ask for clarification or to ask follow up questions.

Boom! Just like that, your window of opportunity to impress or engage with this person has been slammed shut, not by them, but by you.

However, if you were to use less jargon and a more casual tone to say something like, "We provide software that helps small and medium sized businesses reduce internal communication costs by up to 50 percent," the person you are talking with will probably take you more seriously.

At a minimum, that person will have a better understanding of what your USP is, and will be more likely to ask a follow up question about your business.

They may ask, "How does your software do that?" Or, "What kind of internal communications are included in your software?"

That's the whole key, whether you are on the phone, using email, meeting someone at a networking event, or sharing an elevator with a potential client, is to give them just enough information so that they can easily understand your USP and hopefully be intrigued enough to ask a follow up question.

Now, back to the competition question. You might find that there are other companies that offer a similar product or service. In that case, you may need a stronger and more specific USP.

Examples include:

Quickest implementation process

Most intuitive user interface

The only web-based solution

The most durable

The best quality

Whatever your USP, make sure that you try to quantify it with some additional information. For example, "We have the industry's quickest implementation process which is less than 50 percent of the industry standard time." Or, "On average, our products last five years longer than the industry standard."

Adding this extra information about your USP gives it more credibility and makes it easier for your audience to remember what your USP is.

Whatever product or service you are selling, I would encourage you to develop your own personal brand or USP. You want your prospects and clients to know that you will go the extra step and provide a higher level of service than any of your competitors.

This might mean that you are the most knowledgeable in the industry, or that you are incredibly responsive to client requests, or that you insure 100 percent client satisfaction for services that you sell. It might mean that you are good at anticipating client needs, or are good at helping your clients solve problems. It could even be that you are simply that you are an honest and highly likeable person.

Your personal USP combined with your company's USP should be communicated not just through words but also through actions and results. If you can marry the two in a way that differentiates you from the competition and is attractive to your target audience, you will be a force to be reckoned with and well on your way to becoming a sales superstar.

Development Activity

1. Write down your company's USP.
2. Write down a USP for each product or service that you are selling.
3. What do you want your prospects and clients to see as your personal USP?

Understanding Your Prospect

"Seek first to understand, then to be understood." - Stephen Covey

Understanding your prospect's needs, motivations, concerns, and buying processes plays an incredibly important role in your success as a salesperson. Without knowing what your prospect needs, what and who will influence their decision, and what their buying process is, you will find it very difficult to sell anything to your prospect.

Furthermore, if you haven't taken the time to learn this information from your prospect, it is highly unlikely that they will have sufficient trust in you.

For starters, you should never propose something until you have confirmed whether your client actually has a need for it. Doing so sends the message that you care more about getting the sale than helping your client. Doing so is to court distrust and failure.

We have all been approached at one time or another by a salesperson who simply offers one item after another, hoping that they will eventually offer something that we are actually looking to purchase. Their pitches are typically impersonal, annoying, and at their worst, go something like, "Could I interest you in a new suit? How about a pair of shoes? We have a nice selection of watches, how about a watch?"

In a B2B environment, you might have seen salespeople who treat their product offering as a menu and then offer one product after another in the hopes that they will find something we need, or that we will tire and just buy something to get them out the door.

This kind of sales gives the sales profession a bad name and sends most people running in the opposite direction.

Another example is a salesperson that is selling a specific product or service and simply rattles off all the features and benefits of the product, throws in some jabs at the competition, and attempts a close by offering a special price or access to a limited supply.

In cases like this, where the seller hasn't made an effort or taken the time to understand our needs, not only are we typically reluctant to purchase anything from the salesperson or even continue the discussion, our overriding thoughts tend to be focused on how we can get away from the person in the quickest possible manner.

If you'd like to avoid having your prospects flee from you, I suggest that you invest your time and effort to get to know more about them and their needs. It's always easier to learn about a prospect's situation, requirements and buying process if they are the one doing the talking.

As such, I try to limit the time I'm talking to less than half of the meeting's duration. I prefer to ask a mix of closed- and open-ended questions to keep the person I'm meeting with talking and sharing information.

By following this practice you can be sure that you will be gaining important information about your prospect's needs and motivations. Doing so will increase the likelihood that what you propose will be more suitable and appropriate for your prospect, and it will increase the likelihood that what you propose will be accepted.

That said, simply knowing what to put into a proposal isn't enough. You need to understand what factors will influence your prospect's decision.

Factors that can affect a decision may include trust, your company's reputation and financial strength, quality, service, price, risk to the buyer, features and benefits of your product or service, budget limitations, bid and Request for Proposal (RPF) processes, financing options and more.

As a simplistic example, you may well have discovered that your prospect needs a professional copier that can produce 60 copies per minute. However, if you don't uncover the fact that his company only leases new, top name brand equipment, both you and your prospect will be greatly disappointed if you put forward a proposal to purchase a used second-tier model.

Likewise, it's important to know who else is involved in the buying process. Will the procurement team, the CFO, the CTO, or anyone else have to sign off on the purchase? If you leave out anyone who is involved in the decision making process, and your competitor includes them, you will lose out on the deal. So please find out who is involved in the buying process!

One of the reasons many salespeople don't fully understand their client's needs and buying processes is because they are reluctant to ask the right questions. They may feel that these types of questions are an intrusion on the prospect's privacy or that the prospect may react negatively to the questions.

The reality is that, in most cases, these are unfounded concerns. However, in order to ensure that your questions are favorably received, you should script a few and then practice them on a regular basis.

The following are examples of questions that will help you to gain a better understanding of your client and their requirements.

"In order for me to better understand your situation and present the most appropriate solution, would it be alright if I asked a few questions?"

"Would you mind telling me if your decision will be influenced mostly by price, or are there other factors?"

"If you could create the perfect solution, what would it look like?"

"What are your biggest concerns about changing providers?"

"Can you tell me who else will be involved in evaluating our proposal?"

"What would we have to do to make our proposal more attractive to you?"

"Are there any specific issues or challenges that you are currently facing?"

These questions, and ones like these, will be well received by business people or individuals who are seriously in the market for a new product or service. That is because most people want to find a solution that meets their individual or specific needs. And most people understand that sharing information with a potential provider is an important part of that process.

That said, not all the information about your client can or will be revealed in your initial meeting(s). Sometimes you will have to listen to what is not said or look for other verbal and non-verbal cues.

For example, if your prospect is reluctant to give straight answers or if they continually need to consult with others, they may not actually have the buying power. They might tell you or imply that that they are the ultimate decision maker because they may not want to introduce the person who has the real authority.

Likewise, a vendor may reject your proposal without giving you a reason. Sometimes, they will simply put off responding to you in an attempt to reject your proposal and, at the same time, avoid any confrontation or negative feelings. In cases such as these, you should do your best to find the cause for the delay or rejection.

One last thing to keep in mind is that people make decisions differently based on their personalities. Some people place a greater emphasis on personal relationships. Some people are more analytical and simply want to compare and analyze the company and product information. Other people like to be educated and sold to in a systematic and professional manner.

As such, it's important that you try to understand the personality type of the person or people you are dealing with.

Very few people will simply tell you what their buying style is. In fact, they may not even know it themselves. However, if you listen to what they say and observe their actions, you can usually get an idea of how best to communicate with them.

I personally enjoy getting to know my prospects and understanding their needs. Not only is this one of the benefits of working in sales, but it is also one of the things that can greatly accelerate your success.

If you make a sincere effort to know your clients, I'm certain you will be a successful salesperson as well.

Development Activity

After each meeting write down the key factors in your prospect's buying decision, and also include any other people who might be involved in the process.

The Importance of Trust

"Trust is the glue of life. It's the most essential ingredient in effective communication." – Stephen Covey

Trust is one of the most important factors in the great majority of all buying decisions. If your client or prospect trusts you, they will be inclined to do business with you. This will be true even if your pricing is slightly higher than the competition, or if you don't have the most advanced offering on the market.

Think about it. Would you buy a car, a computer, or even a cup of coffee from someone that you didn't trust, just because it was cheap? In the case of the car or the computer, you might save a few dollars, but you would be risking that the products might be damaged, of poor quality, or possibly even stolen.

In the case of the cup of coffee, or any food product for that matter, don't you first have to trust that the seller has done the preparation in a sanitary environment using quality ingredients? If you don't trust the person giving you the food, you probably wouldn't take it, even if it were free.

Of course, we do buy cars, computers, and even coffee from complete strangers. But typically, they are wrapped and presented in the cloak of their company's reputation and credibility.

While we might not know them as individuals, we do trust the car dealer, the computer manufacturer, or the coffee shop. Since the people working there are extensions of these organizations, we trust them too.

You might counter that millions of items are sold and purchased between complete strangers everyday via websites such as eBay, etc. This is a valid observation. However, please keep two things in mind. Buyers on these sites are typically placing a premium on price and/or availability.

Sellers and buyers both have ratings that show the number of transactions they have been involved with and how they have been rated by the people they have concluded transactions with.

In this manner, buyers can choose to pay a slightly higher price to a highly ranked seller. Or, if price and everything else are equal, the buyer can opt to purchase from the seller with the highest rankings. This is, in itself, proof that trust is worth a premium and that all things being equal or almost equal, the party that is trusted will get the deal.

In fact, this is one of the greatest advantages of the Internet and social media. Not only can we research and compare the features, specifications, and benefits of different products, we can also check on the reliability of a product, the manufacturer, and sometimes even the individual who is selling the product.

Trust is arguably even more important in B2B sales. That's where the old adage "Nobody ever got fired for buying IBM," comes into play. Most people prefer to go with a trusted brand and aren't willing to risk their jobs in order to save a few dollars by purchasing an unknown or less reliable brand. Would you?

Trust is very important. In fact, trust is one of the most important factors in the sales process. Be that as it may, you might now be asking, "Then how do you get your prospects and clients to trust you?"

It might seem difficult if you don't have a plan or process. You can't buy trust. You can't rush trust. You have to develop it. You have to earn it and nurture it.

You are probably thinking, "Well then, how do I earn, develop and nurture trust?"

There are many ways to earn and develop trust and they are all complimentary to each other and to the sales process. From the very first contact with your prospect and until the close and follow up, you should always be implementing these methods to continually strengthen the trust your prospects and clients have in you.

When you first contact your prospect, you need to do so in a highly professional manner that gives the impression that you are someone who is good at his or her job and can be trusted. If your initial contact is by email, make sure that it is well written, to the point, and doesn't contain any typos. Definitely check the spelling of your prospect's and their company's name.

Speaking from experience, not only is it embarrassing to get one of these wrong, it's also the equivalent of digging a hole for yourself that takes a fair amount of time and work to climb your way out of.

Likewise, if you first contact is by phone, you need to make your pitch in a concise, and professional manner. State who you are, what your value proposition is, and the reason for your call.

For example, I would say, "Hi, this is Mark Shriner from The Inside Game. We work with many of the leading companies in your industry to help them to improve operational efficiency and become more profitable. I'm calling because I'd like to share some of our latest industry research regarding the latest methods for increasing profits."

From this point, I'd probably ask a couple of questions that would allow me to qualify the person that I was speaking with, get a better understanding of their role and needs, and also demonstrate my professional knowledge. Then, if this person were indeed an appropriate target, I would suggest a meeting.

Once the meeting time and date had been set, I'd send a short introductory email with a reminder of the time, date, location, and subject of the meeting. On the meeting date, I'd show up a few minutes early, dressed in an appropriate manner and fully prepared for the meeting.

Up to this point, I've had opportunities to demonstrate my professionalism and, by extension, my trustworthiness. During the meeting, I can further develop and strengthen the trust by asking insightful questions, demonstrating my empathy for my prospect's needs, and presenting my information in a clear, friendly, and professional manner.

One of the best ways to gain a person's trust is to promise them something by a set time and to deliver by that time or earlier. Doing so demonstrates reliability.

So, at some point during every meeting, I always try to find something that I can promise to provide for my prospect at a later time. This could be some additional industry research, information about the competition, or an introduction to someone that the prospect would like to meet. It could even be something that's not related to work at all.

For example, I've had prospects that expressed an interest in particular holiday destinations, sporting activities and restaurants. I always tell them that I will get back to them with some additional information within two days of our meeting. Then, I simply provide the promised information by the promised time.

This demonstrates that I'm both conscientious and willing to make an extra effort to help my prospect.

One of the most effective ways to develop trust with a prospect is to be favorably introduced by a trusted friend or colleague. When this happens, you automatically inherit some of the trust that your prospect has with the person who introduces you.

Another favorite trust-winning method is to receive a positive testimonial about your product or service from either a satisfied client or well-known industry expert.

As an example, a statement such as, "ABC Company's products have helped our company dramatically reduce costs and improve our operational efficiency. Since using them, we have had a 20 percent improvement in our bottom line," from a respected third party will be more effective at gaining your prospect's trust than if you said the same things yourself.

Likewise, if a trusted industry expert gives public praise to your company's products, customer service, or to you, trust will be more easily gained.

Industry credentials or designations, such as Certified Financial Planner (CFP) and Chartered Financial Consultant (ChFC) can also help establish your credibility and trustworthiness.

Finally, when you conclude a deal and move on to the delivery and implementation stage, it is critical that you try to over deliver, or at least deliver 100 percent of what you have promised. The quality of your product, the quality of your service you provide, and quality of your communications with your client will ultimately have the biggest impact on the level of trust they have in you.

Whatever methods you use, you should continually work to strengthen the trust of your prospects and clients. In addition to the financial rewards that come from being a trusted expert or business partner, having people trust you is also one of the most enjoyable and spiritually rewarding aspects of doing business.

Development Activity

After each meeting ask yourself what you did to increase the trust between you and your prospect or client.

Consultative Selling

"Tell me and I forget, teach me and I may remember, involve me and I learn." – Benjamin Franklin

The movement towards "consultative selling," or "consultative sales" is one of the most important developments in the sales profession. The term can mean different things to different people. But, at its core, it reflects a paradigm shift in terms of how sales people act in front of their prospects and clients. This ultimately goes on to affect how those same prospects and clients perceive the sales professional, and their willingness to trust and place business with them.

Traditionally, salespeople would exert a great amount of time and effort trying to get in front of a prospect. This could be done by various methods including cold calling on the phone and cold calling in person. Once in front of the prospect, the salesperson would typically spend most of the time presenting information about their company and products.

Before personal computers became commonplace, a salesperson might simply read through a company brochure or catalog. In more recent times, Powerpoint presentations, whether printed or on a computer, became the standard. Regardless of the medium, the content was generally the same and would include the following:

1. Company History: date founded, important dates etc.

2. Company Vitals: annual turnover, number of offices, locations, number of staff etc.

3. Product or Service Introduction

More sophisticated versions might include industry trends that demonstrate the importance of the product or service that is being introduced and/or case studies showing how other organizations have benefited from these same products or services.

Regardless of the content, the flow of information was almost entirely from the salesperson towards the prospect. The phrase "show up and throw up" or "SUTU" pretty much captures this approach to sales.

There are several problems with the SUTU approach. For starters, you are entering the relationship as a person who clearly places a greater priority on your desire to sell than on gaining an understanding of your prospect's needs and finding solutions for them.

In short, you are assuming the role and positioning yourself as a typical "salesperson." This in turn makes it difficult for you to gain your prospect's trust or even to uncover useful information that might help you in the sales process.

Secondly, since you haven't taken the time to understand your prospect's needs or concerns, you risk presenting information that is completely irrelevant to them. They might not care about your company history. They might not care about how many offices you have around the world. They might not care about 100 percent of the information in your Powerpoint presentation.

They might, in fact, have a very specific need that they want to discuss with an expert. However, since you have spent most of the time talking and presenting, you won't be able to uncover this need or position yourself as a person that is capable of providing a solution.

The traditional sales approach also places a strong emphasis on overcoming objections and always working for "the close." The problem with immediately overcoming objections is that you are again assuming the role of the traditional salesperson and offering scripted responses to your prospect's concerns.

This can be perceived by your counterpart as an attempt at only persuading them to buy from you. You are clearly putting a priority on your interests as opposed to trying to understand the needs of your prospect. As we will discuss later, it can be much more effective to spend some time acknowledging and exploring the objections that are raised rather than immediately trying to counter them.

Likewise, if you follow the "Always Be Closing" or ABC approach to sales, you risk annoying or scaring off many prospects. Most of the so-called "trial closes," or attempts to maneuver your prospect into placing an order, are seen as poorly disguised attempts at manipulation. Nobody likes to be manipulated and nobody likes to have their intelligence insulted by being the target of such simplistic methods.

When you try to force a close at the end of the meeting, you are again putting the business relationship and your professional image at risk by trying to get your prospect to do something they are not ready to do.

When you use techniques such as offering a "special, one-time only" price, or a access to a "limited supply," or some other attempt at creating urgency, you may, occasionally, win the battle and get the sale. However, in terms of gaining your prospect's trust and repeat business, you will often lose the war.

Please understand that I'm not completely discounting the use of closing techniques nor am I saying they can't be effective. I am simply saying that a more effective and sustainable approach to sales is to focus on first understanding your prospect's needs and then preparing your prospect to make a buying decision. This method is directly opposed to forcing or manipulating prospects into a premature decision.

This is where consultative sales come into play. This approach is all about playing the role of a professional consultant and subject matter expert that willingly puts his or her client's interests ahead of, or at least even with, his or her own.

Think about it. When you are facing a serious challenge, wouldn't you prefer to talk to a professional consultant who is an empathetic listener and has experience with the same kind of challenges, as opposed to a person who is only meeting with you in order to promote their own self-interests?

How does one play the part of professional consultant? First, as we have discussed in an earlier chapter, you must know your product and service inside out. Know all the possible applications, benefits, and even the shortcomings.

Know the same things about your competition. Get to know and understand the most common challenges faced by your clients and prospects as well as many of the most effective solutions for those challenges.

For example, if you are selling to an industry where reduction in fixed overhead costs is driving business decisions, you should be knowledgeable about the most effective strategies that are being adopted. If quality or performance are the critical issues, then become an expert on the leading strategies that are being adopted in those areas.

Having this knowledge allows you to bring much more value to the table when meeting with your clients and will help you to position yourself as a trusted professional resource.

Of course, you shouldn't simply show up at a meeting and start reciting all of the really cool knowledge that you've acquired. It's more effective to demonstrate your knowledge by asking intelligent questions about your prospect's business that serve to help you understand their needs and to show that you understand the industry and the common challenges that are faced by companies in that area.

For example, instead of asking a broad question like, "What challenges are you currently facing?" it would be better to ask a question such as, "How many of your competitors have started to outsource some of their back office operations to specialist firms, and what are your thoughts on this type of strategy?"

Likewise, instead of asking, "What are you doing to improve quality?" you might ask, "How is your firm planning to meet the latest ISO or CE requirements?"

The more questions you ask, the better. The more questions you ask, and the more intelligent and focused those questions are, the better yet.

The information gathered and the good will that you are developing will help you to move towards the next step in the consultative sales process. This is getting your prospect to agree to entertain a proposal.

At some point in the meeting or during the sales process, you will feel that you have enough information to understand what exactly your prospect needs. That's when you should offer to prepare a solution for those needs. It's important how and when you do this.

If you simply throw out possible solutions during the meeting, you risk failure as your client may not understand the benefit of what you are proposing or may feel rushed.

I remember one of my first client meetings as a financial advisor. My prospective client had a significant amount of cash that was just sitting in their checking account. They didn't want to invest in anything that was perceived as being risky, but they did want to get a better rate of a return that they were getting from their bank.

After asking my client a few questions about their situation and what it is they would like to do, I started to offer up, one by one, some possible solutions.

"How about a CD that will earn five percent interest." "No? Then how about a money market fund with a slightly lower rate but that is very liquid?" "No? Well then, how about some cash value life insurance?"

My prospect balked at all three of these "solutions" and several others that I continued to throw out in rapid-fire succession.

Not only had I failed to demonstrate my willingness to listen and understand my client's needs, I had thrown out several possible solutions without getting my prospect permission to do so.

When I did make suggestions for possible solutions, I did so without explaining my rationale or the characteristics and benefits of each solution. In fact, I mistakenly took it for granted that my prospect would understand what I was proposing and why.

In retrospect, it would have been better for me to recap what my client had told me, thus demonstrating that I had both listened to and understood what my client had shared with me. I could have then offered to put together a suitable proposal.

I could have said, "What I'm hearing is that you aren't really happy with the rate of return you're getting from the bank on the cash in your checking account. You'd like to earn some additional interest on that money, but you don't want to be exposed to too much risk. Is that accurate?"

After receiving confirmation from my prospect, I could have then offered to put together a suitable proposal based upon their requirements.

For example, "Based on what you've told me, I'm confident that we have at least a couple of different options that will meet your needs. Would it be okay for me to do a little more research back at the office to make sure that the programs I have in mind are the most appropriate for you, and then come back to you with a cash management plan that is tailored for your requirements?"

In this case, it may seem that I have slowed the selling process down a bit. However, by asking for the client to verify my understanding of their needs and by asking their permission to prepare a proposal or plan, I have actually brought them further into the consultative process.

I have also set the stage for the next meeting. Not only will they be expecting to listen to my proposal, as opposed to me mostly listening to them, they should be somewhat excited or at least intrigued to hear what I will be proposing.

This mindset will give me the opening I need to explain the reasons I've proposed what I have and the benefits for the client.

In the case of the client in the example above, I would start the next meeting by briefly recapping what they had told me in the previous meeting. I would then introduce a couple of solutions, explain the features and benefits of each one, explain how these solutions meet their requirements, and what, if any, detractors there were.

I might even show a chart to make any comparisons easier and to show that I have done my homework and have worked to find the best solution for my client.

As I mentioned, when you offer to come back with a well thought out proposal, it can create a sense of anticipation in your client. They will be looking forward to seeing your proposal. This is because they really do want their problem solved. They want a solution and are in some ways mentally rooting for you to deliver it.

Often times, in B2B situations, I will play this anticipation up even more. For example, I may stress that we will be presenting something very unique or special at the meeting. Or I'd say that we are developing a custom solution specifically for the client that will not only meet their needs but also give them a competitive advantage.

Of course, if your company doesn't have something that will meet your prospect's needs, you shouldn't be dishonest about it. In cases like this, you may feel like the situation is a lost cause. I assure you that, often times, it's not.

I have found that some of my biggest successes have come from being direct and honest with my prospect and ending a meeting with this, "Based upon what you've shared with me, I don't think any of the services that I previously had in mind would be a good match. I do have some ideas though. Would it be alright for me to go back and check with my team? If we can come up with an appropriate solution that can help you achieve your targets, then we can set up another meeting?"

By closing a meeting like this, I have taken all the pressure off the prospect who, regardless of how well the meeting went, may still have had their guard up against closing attempts. Additionally, I have planted the seeds of both anticipation and the prospect's willingness to accept a future meeting request.

I may have also gained some credibility and respect. This is simply because I have been honest with my client, and almost everyone values and respects honesty.

In fact, I've never been refused on this request or on a subsequent follow-up meeting request. What has happened often is that my prospect anticipated my call and eagerly invited me back to see what solution we have come up with.

When you do go back with your proposal, remember to recap what has been discussed in the previous meeting and ask your prospect if your summary is accurate or if they would like to add anything.

When presenting the proposal, be sure to stress the benefits to your prospect and how each element aligns with one of their stated requirements. The benefits and connection to the client's needs may seem clear to you, but it never hurts to make sure of what is being communicated.

Lastly, one thing you might consider is explaining your sales approach with your prospect at the outset of the first meeting. For example, you might explain that you follow a consultative process that begins with conducting a needs analysis, followed by a proposal, then implementation of the proposal, followed by regular reviews of the effectiveness of what has been purchased and understanding any new issues or needs.

By doing this, you are letting your prospect know what to expect. Furthermore, you are not only directing the meeting as discussed in an earlier chapter, but you are also directing the relationship and sales process with your client.

If your prospect agrees to participate in the process with you, you have taken a major step towards converting that prospect into a client. This is because they actively become part of the process and they actually want you to help them find an appropriate solution.

Development Activity

Write a detailed explanation of your sales process that will help you explain to your clients what they should expect from you.

Closing Made Easy

"Always be closing...That doesn't mean you're always closing the deal. But it does mean that you need to be always closing on the next step in the process." – Shane Gibson

"However beautiful the strategy, you should occasionally look at the results." – Winston Churchill

For as long as there have been salespeople, there has also been concern about, and a large importance placed on, "closing." The famous and oft used expression "always be closing," or "ABC" is known by most business people whether or not they are involved in sales. This, in itself, is a testament to the importance that sales people place on closing the deal.

In this chapter, we will discuss a couple of different mindsets related to closing and also look at some of the more commonly used techniques. As we do so, please keep in mind that there really is no one single best technique or method to close a deal. It really comes down to what is most appropriate given the product or service you are selling, the type of prospect you are dealing with, and what best fits your sales style.

With that in mind, let me start by saying that I believe there has been too much focus placed on getting to the close in traditional sales literature.

Of course, you can't convert prospects into clients without closing. However, if you are always going for the close, the people you are selling to will immediately sense this. As a result, it will be difficult for you to gain their trust, and ultimately, their business.

Since it's a common stereotype that salespeople are always going for the close, the people you are selling to are often expecting that you will try to push them into a buying decision. In fact, they may even be on the lookout for attempted closes, and at the first sign of one, will be ready to put forth an objection or use an alternative way find a way not to be closed.

At some point the buying decision can be subverted into a psychological tug of war between you and your prospect. Your prospect may dig in their heels and not allow themselves to be "closed" because, to them, it feels that they are somehow being coerced into a deal.

And, as most people really don't like to feel that they have been manipulated or forced into something, your prospect may simply refuse to buy from you because doing so would give them that feeling.

So, whatever technique or process you adopt, please try your best to avoid giving your prospect the impression that they are being led or forced into a close. Don't follow some of the more crude and obvious closing methods.

Let's look at some the most common approaches to closing. One, as already mentioned, is the traditional mindset and approach that we should always be closing. That is, a salesperson should continually look for opportunities to close the deal.

For example, during a meeting a salesperson might continually attempt trial closes such as, "If we were able to meet your requirements, would you be able to move forward today?" Or, "This package is exactly what you've described, should I go ahead and reserve it for you?"

If a prospect, agrees, out comes the paperwork and the deal moves to conclusion. If the prospect disagrees, they will be asked to state their rationale for saying no. Then, the conversation can rapidly turn into a battle of objections and counters to overcome the stated objections.

Typically this approach is used for lower cost items or subscription services such as cable TV, mobile phone services, or health club memberships. It is also commonly used by salespeople who are selling items such time-share condominiums, or vacation properties. This approach is sometimes categorized as a "high-pressure" sales tactic.

In these cases the salesperson is primarily concerned with closing as many deals as possible in the shortest amount of time. When used for these purposes to sell the above-mentioned types of products, this method can be quite effective.

From the prospect's perspective, being sold to in this manner can be quite tiring as they either need to make a buying commitment or they are forced to defend the reasons for not buying.

On the other hand, when this approach is performed well, it can seem more like the salesperson is simply checking and confirming the prospect's requirements.

For example, questions such as the following might be used:

"Is there anything else that we could include that would make this a more attractive order?"

"Is there anything we can do to improve this offer?"

"Is there anything stopping you from moving forward?"

Once the prospect has answered any of these questions, you can follow up with, "If we can meet your requirements, would you be okay to move forward?"

What you are trying to do is get your prospect to state their rational requirements for the product or service that you are selling. By doing so, you can help to remove some of the emotional or seemingly irrational factors that can influence a buying decision.

You are not trying to lead your prospect into a close, or corner them. If you meet the prospect's stated requirements and they still refuse to buy, you can't simply confront them with something like, "But Bob, you said that if I gave you this package you would buy. Why aren't you buying?"

This will immediately give your prospect the correct feeling that you aren't to be trusted, that you care more about the close than about your prospect's needs, and that you have attempted to trap them into making a buying decision.

Few people will buy from someone that they don't trust regardless of whether the product or service is attractive. So, just because you have gotten your prospect to put all their requirements on the table, don't think you can ignore factors such as trust, and just march directly to a forced close.

A better approach would be to follow up with, "Can you help me understand how I can make this offer more appropriate for you?" Or, you could try, "Is there anything else we can do to make this package more suitable for you?" In these cases, you are asking for more information about your prospect's requirements and thus demonstrating that you want to find the best solution for them.

Again, in my opinion, this approach is best suited for lower cost products and services where there are fewer factors and fewer people involved in the buying process. Or, if you are only interested in doing one deal with the prospect and don't expect any future referrals from them, being an aggressive closer may make sense.

Another commonly accepted approach says that closing should be part of a larger sales process and only attempted after a certain milestone has been reached.

For example, financial advisors often times will have a sales process that has several steps and goals for each step such as:

1. Initial meeting (build rapport, explain financial advisor's process, complete needs analysis or financial review questionnaire)

2. Second meeting (discuss results of needs analysis, propose financial plan)*

3. Third meeting (open account, implement plan)

4. Fourth meeting (review financial situation and the performance of the existing financial plan, propose modifications to the plan).**

The first close would be attempted at the end of Stage 2

**Additional closes for new businesses would be attempted at Stage 4 and during subsequent review meetings.*

In the above example, it wouldn't make sense for the financial advisor to try to close the deal before they have fully understood their prospect's needs or fully explained to the prospect why are they proposing a specific plan. Doing so would cause the advisor to run the risk of both proposing the wrong solution and destroying the advisor's credibility with their prospect.

This approach is also more common in B2B sales situations with larger ticket times. Again, generally speaking, you can't sell something to a business until you have understood what their requirements are and what would be the most appropriate product or service to meet those requirements. And, you can rarely get a business to spend money on a product or service that that it simply doesn't need.

So forget about the forced close. Instead, try to get your prospect to agree to participate with you in a transparent and predefined process that will include a proposal step. This will lead you and your prospect towards the close. When the time comes for you to deliver your proposal, it will not only be accepted, it will be welcomed.

This process can, and should be, tailored to make it suitable to the product or service you are selling. For example, if you are selling something with a short sales cycle that doesn't require the participation of multiple decision makers, you can keep the process short and simple.

However, if you are selling a product or service that involves multiple decision makers, requires product demos or trials, and a more complicated needs analysis, you will need to take all these factors into consideration and include them in the process.

To kick things off, you need to get your prospect's buy-in to, and participation in, the process. For a simple process, you can typically define it yourself and ask for your prospect to agree.

For example, you could say, "We typically like to get an understanding of our client's requirements and come back with a proposal. Would that approach be okay with you?"

Or, "In order for me to show how best we might be able to help you lower your costs/improve your quality/reduce your turn-around-times, would it be alright for me to ask you some questions?

In more complicated situations, you will want to explain to your prospect that preparing the most appropriate solution requires the commitment of time and resources on your side and can only be successful if both sides work together.

For example, "In order for us to conduct a detailed needs analysis, develop an appropriate solution and run an on-site trial, we will have to invest a fair amount of our time and resources. In order to justify that investment and to ensure that we develop the most appropriate solution, we ask that our clients work with us to define this process. Would that approach make sense to you?"

When the prospect agrees, you would then follow up with a joint document that has all the steps and deliverables defined, dates attached, and a list of all involved parties from both companies for each step.

For example, if you need to involve people from the finance or IT departments in some stages of the process, it's much better to learn about that at the outset and plan for it than to find out later on. The process document not only helps you to gain an understanding of these requirements in advance, it also helps to take a lot of the guesswork out of what the next steps will be and when they will occur.

Once you have mutually agreed on a process with all stakeholders noted and participating, you simply have to follow that process and conduct your close at the agreed stage.

Now, even though I've just said that businesses can't be pushed into a close and should follow a planned process in order to conclude deals, I'm going to talk about some ways that can actually accelerate movement to the close.

These approaches can resemble some of the higher-pressure techniques that I had earlier discouraged. But, when used at the right time in an appropriate manner, they can be highly effective.

Both of these techniques involve creating a sense of urgency with your prospect. For example, if there is a booking deadline or a cut-off date for an attractive price or package deal, your prospect will feel the need to commit by that time. Or, if you have limited stock or supply of a popular product or service, you can use that to get your prospect to buy now.

For example, trade show organizers will offer the premium booth space to exhibitors who reserve their space early on. On the other hand, if there are only a few spaces left, exhibitors will often sign on the spot simply because they don't want to be left out of the event.

As stated before, buyers don't like to be pushed into a deal. However, if the deadlines are real, and there really are limited stocks, supplies, or spaces, people generally prefer to be informed and offered the option of buying now.

Here's one last thought about closing. Many salespeople, especially less experienced ones, will feel uncomfortable asking their prospects to buy their service and conclude the deal. They have no problem presenting and learning about their prospect's requirements. However, when it comes to asking for a buying commitment, they lack confidence and aren't sure how to proceed.

The best way to prevent this from happening is to plan your approach in advance and practice it. That way, when the time comes to ask for the order, you will do so in a confident and natural manner.

Personally, in addition to getting my prospect to agree to a pre-defined process, I typically like to close the deal by using slightly less direct language than simply asking for the person to sign a contract. I might say something like, "We just need to complete an order form and then we can move to the next step," or "If I can just get you to initial this order form, I will make sure that we start to prepare everything immediately."

The point is you don't have create a lot of drama around asking someone to sign a formal contract. If a contract is required, you should present it in a matter-of-fact manner after the deal has been closed by getting verbal or written confirmation of the terms in advance.

Ask For The Samples

Early on in my sales career I was selling advertising for a leading print and online B2B media company. Our magazines and websites helped to promote the products of manufacturers to large overseas importers.

I had no problem confidently introducing our services, but I couldn't tell when I should try to close the deal or what I should even say.

I asked one of our top salespeople how he could tell when a prospect was ready to sign. He told me that whenever a prospect would provide him with their product samples to be used in the creation of an advertisement or company website, he knew that they were serious and ready to sign an advertising agreement.

From that day forward, I made it part of my closing process to simply ask the prospective client for their product samples so that I could prepare their company's web catalog. If they agreed, I presented the contract at that time.

This turned into a winning approach for me as I felt much more comfortable asking for their product samples than directly asking for them to sign a contract. In the end, the result was the same, i.e. I got the deal. But the approach I had adopted felt much smoother to me and resulted in more self-confidence when closing. It also resulted in me winning a lot more business.

Regardless of what style or process you adopt to close deals, you should make sure that you know about any internal process and document requirements of your company in advance.

For example, most life insurance and financial services companies require a fair number of documents and disclosures to be signed by your client. They also require a legal ID, proof of address, and may also require health checks and possibly even signatures of spouses.

You definitely need to know all of this in advance so you can accurately explain the process and requirements to your clients. You may even want to plan and practice how you will explain these steps and how you will guide your client through them.

If you don't, you run the risk of both giving and receiving an unwelcome surprise. In life insurance sales, I've seen several deals go south and get put on hold because the client wasn't aware that a medical check would be required, or because a spouse wasn't included in the sales discussion and then refused to sign because she felt that she had been left out of an important financial decision.

At the same time, I've seen financial advisors who weren't aware of certain document filing requirements and then had to forfeit commissions because the company couldn't process the already completed deal.

Regardless of your industry or company, there will be some sort of standard internal process and document requirements. Make sure you know them, are comfortable presenting them, and have a well-thought strategy for getting them completed.

In closing (pun intended!), whatever product or service you are selling, you should figure out the approach that that is most appropriate for you and your prospects, and then practice it until it becomes a natural part of your sales process.

Development Activity

1. Identify when is the best time to attempt to close deals in your selling process.
2. Identify the approach you will take.
3. Prepare and practice all the related language and support materials for your approach. (e.g. What exactly will you say? What documents will you need? Etc.)

Lead Generation

"Don't judge each day by the harvest you reap but by the seeds that you plant." – Robert Louis Stevenson

One of the most important factors in the success of any salesperson or sales organization is the quantity and quality of leads that they are able to generate. If you don't have a strategy or multiple strategies for generating leads, the growth of your sales pipeline will be greatly hindered and your success or failure will occur in a seemingly more random manner.

If you would like to remove the randomness from your ability to succeed in sales, you need to stack the cards in your favor. This can most effectively done by ensuring that you are continually receiving high quality sales leads.

There are multiple methods used by leading sales professionals and organizations to ensure the continual generation of leads. These include advertising, trade show participation, online marketing, social media, content marketing, public speaking, participating in networking events and business organizations, affiliate marketing, partnering with centers of influence, and referrals.

This chapter will provide an overview of these methods. But, we will focus more on the activities that can be easily implemented by individual sales people and that are not dependent on marketing departments or advertising budgets.

That said, we will still touch on many of these more strategic methods used by companies as it is important for salespeople to have an understanding of larger lead generation strategies that their organizations may be able to implement.

As an individual salesperson, or as a sales team, you should continually be developing leads in the form of referrals from satisfied clients, trusting prospects, and sometimes, depending on the type of service you are selling, even friends and family.

For corporate B2B sales, there are a couple of distinct classifications of referrals and, correspondingly, there are distinct methods for requesting them. You can think about referrals inside an existing customer's organization as one type, and referrals to people in outside organizations as a second type.

As I have often worked in regional roles covering several countries, one of my favorite techniques for pursuing referrals inside of a specific organization involves asking a satisfied customer for an introduction to a colleague in another geographic area.

My request is usually something like this, "By the way, I'll be in New York next week for a couple of business meetings. Would you happen to know someone in your marketing department there that I could reach out to?"

More often than not, this approach is successful as the request is reasonable and really isn't a great imposition on my client. I haven't asked for an endorsement or a referral, I've simply asked for a name or a connection. This approach can work across regions or even across departments.

For example, I could ask to be connected to someone in the procurement department, in the HR department, etc. The important thing is that I am leveraging my relationship with one person or one department to open the door to another person or another department.

This is much more effective than cold calling or sending unsolicited emails, as people are typically much more willing to speak with someone that was referred by a colleague or someone they know. An introduction from a trusted person also accelerates the acquisition of trust.

Timing referral requests to correspond with business travel can be effective as people are often more willing to meet with a person if they know that he or she is visiting from another location and will only be in their area for a limited amount of time.

If you are in the business of providing a service to individuals, for example as a real estate agent or a financial advisor, you should always be looking for opportunities to ask for an introduction or a referral.

I say you should look for an opportunity because you will want to make your requests at an appropriate time. If you happen to ask at an inappropriate time, not only will you probably not receive a referral, you may run the risk of damaging the relationship with the person you are asking. The best time to ask for a referral is after you have delivered value to your client and they have acknowledged the work you have done.

For example, if you have just helped someone sell their home and they are thanking you for the job you have done, you might want to say something like, "I've really enjoyed working with you too. If you don't mind, I do have one request. If you happen to know anyone who's thinking about buying or selling a home, and you think that I might be able to help, could you please let me know?"

The odds are that at any given time, the person you are talking with will probably not be able to think of anyone. But, you never know. Sometimes, you will receive an immediate intro. The important thing is that you ask enough people at the appropriate time.

By doing this, you are planting the seeds for current and future opportunities. And when you've received a positive response from your client, it's important that you follow up on a regular basis to "water" those seeds, and remind them of your service and their commitment making referrals when appropriate.

Follow up can be done by sending cards, calendars, market updates etc. You don't need to bombard you referral sources too frequently or forcefully. In my experience 9-12 "touches" via email, post cards, phone calls, meetings, etc. per year is enough for most people to keep you mind for appropriate opportunities.

I have found that networking events, chamber of commerce and other business association meetings can be a great source for getting to know new people, learning about a variety of topics, and, when effectively utilized, an important source of high quality leads.

I'd like to stress the importance of effective participation in events. You can't simply show up and expect the other attendees to start sending you business. This can happen, but it's not usually the way it works.

You should have a strategy of not just attending events, but actively participating in them. If possible, introduce yourself to the organizers in advance. You might even ask if they need any volunteers for this or future events.

Even if you don't volunteer, make sure you know who the leaders are and make sure you reintroduce yourself at the event. Get to know the organizers. Ask them how they got involved in this particular organization or event, and find out what other activities and organizations they are involved in.

Once you have done this, you will find that good organizers will often start to introduce you to other leaders and attendees at the event. If this doesn't happen on it's own, don't be afraid to ask for an introduction to a particular person or company at the event.

When you are at an event, don't try to sell to the people you meet. That's not your mission. Your mission should be to expand your network and increase the number of referral sources you have. To do this, try your best to get to know as many people as possible.

This doesn't mean that you "speed network" to get as many business cards as you can. It means to really try to get know people, understand what they do, why they are at the event, and possibly even learn about some of their personal interests.

People like meeting those who show a sincere interest in other people's work and interests. Most people don't like to be sold to. Focus on learning about the other attendees and you will make a much better impression than you would if you simply approached everyone and gave them your elevator speech and a business card.

Once you have done this with a few people at the event, you will often times be able to start connecting the other attendees. For example, you might connect two people who are avid golfers. Or, you might discover that one person is looking to meet someone from a particular company or industry that you've already met.

This is when networking can really start to be both fun and productive. As you start to introduce people, you take on the role of a facilitator and start to become more visible and appreciated by the other attendees.

Another way to become more visible, and even trusted, is to be one of the speakers. By giving a presentation on a particular topic, you immediately gain an additional layer of credibility, both in terms of the topic you are speaking about and in terms of your affiliation with the event organization.

Pay attention the next time you attend an event that includes a presentation. Afterwards, you will see that a number of people gravitate towards the speaker to introduce themselves, ask questions, exchange cards, and often times to talk about both additional speaking and business opportunities.

Whether you are an organizer, a speaker, an active facilitator, or just an attendee, proper post-event follow up is important. You can't simply leave, put the business cards in your desk, and expect people to contact you or refer others to you.

You need to follow up with the people you have met. To do this, you should end every conversation at the event with a request for permission to follow up with the individual you had been speaking with. For example, you could simply say, "Mary, it's been nice meeting you. I haven't told you much about what we do. Would it be alright if I email you some information about our services?"

Alternatively, if you have learned about a person's professional or personal interest, you might offer to send them some information on that topic. This could be a research report, a white paper, a link to a relevant website, or information about an upcoming event.

Unless the person has specifically asked me about my company or services, or unless I think they are a good prospect for our services, I typically prefer the second option. This is my way of providing value and being of service to others. There is no real need to pursue business with people who aren't interested in or aren't legitimate prospects for my services.

Post-event follow up might also include some type of social media activity as well. The best and typically most appropriate example is connecting with the other attendees on LinkedIn. This makes it easier for you to keep in touch with others. And when you post links to interesting information, the people you are connected to will sometimes share it with their network as well, thus expanding your reach and the number of potential referral sources.

A Great Networking Experience

Can business networking be both fun and productive? Absolutely!

A good example is what happened to me at a recent event in Tokyo hosted by the American Chamber of Commerce Japan. There were about 150 business people at the event. As soon as I arrived I had a chance to meet and have conversations with the lead organizer and the venue host.

About 30 minutes into the event there was a drawing, and I happened to win the grand prize, a bay view room at the Hilton Conrad Tokyo inclusive of breakfast for two. Wow! That was the beginning of the fun.

From that point on, I had many people come up to congratulate me on my prize, which made it easy for me to get to know them. That in turn made it easy for me to play the role of facilitator. In less than an hour, I was able to bring up a couple of job opportunities to someone who had been looking to change companies, connect two people who were formerly from Denver but now living in Tokyo, and introduce a potential client to a colleague of mine who was also at the event.

To top off the evening, I was approached by the County Manager of a large U.S. IT company. Once he learned about the services my company provided, he asked me to immediately follow up with his head of marketing as his company had an urgent need for our services.

Yes, networking can be both fun and effective!

At the beginning of this chapter, I mentioned advertising, content marketing and exhibition participation as effective methods of lead generation for companies. These activities typically require investment, planning, and the participation of an organization's marketing department. As such, I will just give a brief overview of each and explain their relevance for an individual sales person.

Events, such as trade shows and exhibitions, can be a great way for a company to reach a large number of potential buyers. For, example, a hardware manufacturer might be able generate multiple leads by having a booth at a hardware exhibition that attracts a large number of volume hardware buyers. The same is true for almost any product or service.

The key is to review the attendee list from previous events and see if the people who attend match up with your target customer profile. You will also want to have a strategy that allows you to attract potential buyers to your booth and get them to share their contact details with you. Some exhibition organizers will provide the complete attendee list to exhibitors after the event.

Along with having a solid event strategy, you will need to properly budget your costs for the event. In addition to renting the space, you will need to put up a booth. You may also need to print brochures, create a display, rent or use a computer and an LCD projector.

You might want to bring samples or gifts that will require time to produce and money to ship. You will also need to budget in costs for travel, lodging, meals, and possibly entertainment.

All in, the actual cost of participating in an exhibition can easily be 2 to 3 times the cost of the booth space. But if you get any orders for your product or services at the event or afterwards, you may easily realize a return on that investment.

As with all sales and lead generation activities, proper follow up is essential.

Advertising, print and online, as well as content marketing are more straightforward in their costs and planning. You simply need to find a publication or website that has a readership that matches your target customer profile and then decide on a package that best meets your needs and budget.

With advertising, you place or post an ad that hopefully compels readers to inquire about your products or services. Your unique selling point (USP) and your call to action should be strong and clear.

With content marketing, you don't simply post an ad and hope to be discovered. You place information such as market research or white papers that contain information that will be useful or even valuable to your target audience on a site or newsletter that is read by the companies and individuals you are targeting.

In order to download the complete report or white paper, the reader needs to provide their contact details, which typically include name, email, title and company name. Those details are then provided to you.

This method requires a bit more work in terms of content creation. However, the leads that are generated are typically of higher quality than those received by general advertising.

The lead generation methods mentioned in this chapter are some of the most commonly used and most effective ways for individuals and organizations to generate leads. You don't have to use all of these, and you may use other methods not mentioned here. However, you should, no matter what, have a lead generation strategy in place that you systematically and continually follow.

Case Study: Lead Generation Strategies

The following short case study highlights both the potential benefits and the missed opportunities that can come with either implementing a lead generation strategy, or choosing not have one.

Companies A and B had been competing in the same industry for many years. Their products were very similar in terms of features, quality and price.

Both companies had an active sales force of 15 salespeople. The sales managers in both companies felt that their respective company's success or failure was largely due to the performance of the company's sales team.

At the beginning of the year, Company A decided that, in order to improve the performance of its sales team, it would implement a multi-pronged lead generation strategy that would include both individual activities and company-directed activities.

Company B, on the other hand, decided to invest in adding two salespeople to its team.

For both companies the extra investment equaled approximately $150,000.

Company A coached its salespeople about how to ask for referrals and introductions, how to participate in networking events, and how to use LinkedIn to find prospects and generate leads.

Most of these activities didn't cost any money. However, the company did agree to pay for the participation in networking events. As each rep attended two events per month at $15 per event, the totally annual expense for this activity was around $ 4,600.

The number of leads generated was impressive. As each sales rep typically had two prospect and client meetings per day, they were able to ask around 10 people a week for introductions to colleagues in other locations or in other departments.

Even though only 20 percent of the requests resulted in an introduction, the end result was fantastic. With 15 people asking 10 people a week there were approximately 600 requests per month.

Even with only 20 percent of the requests being successful, Company A's sales team was now generating over 120 new leads per month, or almost 1,500 new leads per year.

On top of that, each salesperson typically received a couple of leads per month from the events they attended and from their social media activity. These provided another 360 leads for the year.

Even though it typically takes time to convert leads into revenues, the leads generated by the individual activities of Company A's sales reps resulted in over $1,500,000 in new business during that first year.

Company A also decided to attend two leading industry exhibitions during the year. With booth space and all other related costs, the total budget for the two exhibitions was $75,000. At each event the participating sales reps from company met with over 300 people.

Of this group only about one third were actual prospects, but they were very high quality in terms of the likelihood of buying. In total there were 200 high quality leads generated from the two shows. Revenues generated from these leads came to around $300,000.

Company A's remaining budget was spent on Google AdWords and online content marketing as lead generation activities.

The AdWords campaign resulted in an average of two leads per day. Many of these leads were poor quality. That is, the person inquiring either wasn't seriously in the market for Company A's product or they weren't qualified to buy. But during the 12-month campaign, leads came in from a few large buying organizations that resulted in orders of over $350,000.

The content marketing strategy generated less than 100 leads. But most were from qualified and interested buyers. These leads resulted in initial orders of over $300,000.

Company A Results
Total Investment: $ 150,000
Total Leads Generated: 2,400 +
Revenues from Lead Generation: $ 2,450,000

Company B Results

The two new salespeople took 2-3 months to ramp up and start selling. For prospecting, they called lists of existing prospects, old clients, and companies from a newly purchased database. All leads were results of direct contact with a prospect.

Both new salespeople managed to generate US$ 400,000 in sales from approximately 10 clients each over their first twelve months.

Total Investment:	$ 150,000
Revenues Generated:	$ 800,000

In conclusion, Company A's results had an ROI three times higher than Company B's. And, possibly even more beneficial, Company A's efforts resulted in over 2,400 leads, many of which will be converted to paying customers in the future.

For those of you that don't belong to a large sales organization, or that don't have an individual budget to spend on exhibitions, advertising, and online lead generation activities, please pay attention to the breakdown of leads and revenues generated. The low-cost individual activities actually generated majority of the leads and the revenues.

Of course, this was the total result of 15 different sales reps. But, you can clearly see that basic activities such as asking for introductions, participating in networking events, and using some free social media sites can increase leads and revenues.

I often coach sales people that are reluctant to ask for introductions or referrals. The most common reason given is that they don't want to impose on their clients and run the risk of damaging their relationship.

I understand that rationale. However, I would say that if you make the request in the appropriate manner and at the appropriate time, you will often find that the person you are asking is very willing to help you. The following is a true story that demonstrates the power and benefit of simply asking for help.

A few years ago I was based in Singapore and working as the Regional Managing Director in Asia for a European multinational company. I had just appointed a new GM for our Hong Kong office and wanted to help him rapidly increase revenues in that office. So prior to his departure for Hong Kong I asked several people for their assistance.

One person, a senior executive at one of the world's largest banks, was someone that I'd only met once before. However, he and my new Hong Kong GM shared the same nationality.

I sent the senior executive an email explaining that one of my staff, who happened to be from the same country as him, was moving into a new role in Hong Kong. I wrote that we would appreciate an opportunity to meet in order to get his advice about managing a business in Hong Kong.

The senior executive agreed and invited us to his office later that week. The meeting started with some casual small talk. However, after about five minutes, the senior executive pulled out his notebook and started giving us the names and contact details for several of his high-ranking colleagues in Hong Kong. He told us to contact them and to say that he had introduced us.

One of his colleagues was the chief operating officer (COO) for the company's investment bank in Hong Kong. When we contacted her, she agreed to meet with us as soon as our new GM arrived in Hong Kong. When we did meet her, we found out that she was ready to change service providers and asked us for a proposal.

Things went well and we received our first order two months later. Within a year, that bank became our largest client in Hong Kong and helped to dramatically increase revenues.

It was an amazing success story that was made possible by a simple request for help.

Development Activity

Create a lead generation strategy that provides at least two regular sources of leads for your business.

The Importance of Motivation

"Success consists of going from failure to failure without the loss of enthusiasm." – Winston Churchill

In most activities, and especially in sales, staying properly motivated is a key ingredient to success. Motivation is the fuel that propels us forward, keeps us enthusiastic, and allows us to overcome whatever obstacles we encounter.

One of the biggest challenges faced by both beginning and experienced salespeople is to continually stay motivated and enthusiastic about their work. The challenge comes from the nature of the job, which, for the great majority, requires us to get through a lot of no's before we get to a yes.

Getting rejected by prospects on the phone, in email, and in person can emotionally drag us down if we aren't mentally prepared and if we don't have a plan to maintain our motivation. Without the proper motivation, it's almost impossible to remain enthusiastic.

Once the motivation and enthusiasm start to take a dive, the natural response of most people is to start doubting themselves, their company, their product, and the market that they are selling into. And, if allowed to solidify, the doubts can turn into fears that result in greater self-doubt, reduced selling activities, and ultimately, failure.

I'm sure that most of us have experienced doing a job when motivated and then doing the same job when we had lost the motivation. It's infinitely easier to work, exercise, study, and practice an activity when we are properly motivated. Sometimes, it can be almost effortless and seem to be a joy.

However, when the motivation is gone, it can feel like you are lifting a ton of bricks just to open a book, put on your running shoes, or pick up the phone and make that cold call.

Clearly this is an unpleasant outcome and one that we would all like to avoid. In order to do so, we need to become aware of the importance of motivation, know the signs that it may be taking a hit, and have a plan in place to continually maintain, support, and even feed and increase it.

How do we do this? It starts with the acknowledgement that staying motivated is critically important to our success and to our happiness. I think we all know this at some level. But not many people recognize that it is something that requires a conscious effort and a plan to accomplish.

We tend to think that we've lost our motivation, or that it's difficult to stay motivated. We may occasionally read some uplifting article, or listen to a motivational speaker. But these are stopgap methods that, while helping for a short time, won't be of much help in the longer-term day-to-day to effort to stay motivated.

Once we acknowledge that staying motivated is important, and that staying motivated requires a plan and regular work, we are halfway home. We just need put together the plan and stick to it.

What does a motivational development plan look like? It may be different for everyone. However, it should start with a clear understanding of why, exactly, you are doing your job or whatever task it is that you want to stay motivated about. In short, what is it that you really want to achieve?

Oftentimes people may think that what they really want is something like a promotion, more money or more free time. But, usually, these are just means to an end. They are more of an abstraction of what it is that we are really aiming to achieve.

If you are working towards a goal that isn't clearly defined or is misrepresented by something else, it's easy to become disillusioned. After a particularly hard day, week, or month, when you are feeling that some of your goals may be out of reach, you may start to tell yourself that you don't really need the promotion, the extra money, or the extra time off.

To prevent yourself from falling into this trap, first get an understanding of what it is exactly that you want to achieve. If more money is your target, ask yourself what you would do with that money. Likewise, if you want more time or a promotion, ask yourself why these are important you.

The answers to these questions are the real reason you are working so hard and are the real motivators for your success. Write these answers down. Visualize them. Whenever you are feeling tired or starting to lose motivation, come back to these reasons.

> "A creative man is motivated by the desire to achieve, not by the desire to beat others." – Ayn Rand

For example, don't think in terms of simply wanting to make more money or have more free time. Think in terms of what exactly you would do with that extra money and time. Visualize yourself doing these things and imagine how good you will feel. Bring that positive imagery and feeling into the moment and use it to motivate you through whatever challenge you may be facing.

Your motivation plan should also include both internal and external sources of motivation. External sources of motivation include regularly reading motivational literature, listening to motivational speakers, and surrounding yourself with positive motivational people.

Internal behaviors that protect our motivation include understanding the importance of motivation, understanding that it can be developed and that seemingly negative things that happen to us don't necessarily need to bring us down. Understanding and reflecting on the real reasons you are pursuing your goals is another important internal source of motivation.

For the external sources, you might want to start and finish each day by reading some motivational literature or quotes. For example, if I read a few pages written by writers such as Stephen R. Covey, Napoleon Hill, Benjamin Franklin or Tony Robbins, it usually has an immediate positive impact on my state of mind. It helps to fuel up and edify my motivation.

Likewise, if I am without a book, I can simply go online and search for motivational or inspirational quotes. Just this morning, I did this and found hundreds of positive and inspirational messages from some of the world's greatest thinkers, performers and humanitarians. Examples include:

"Always do your best. What you plant now, you will harvest later."
- Og Mandino

"Be kind whenever possible. It is always possible." – Dalai Lama

"The secret to getting ahead is getting started." – Mark Twain

"Start where you are. Use what you have. Do what you can." – Arthur Ashe

I love starting the day with a couple of positive and motivational messages bouncing around in my mind. I usually try to find a message that somehow relates to a specific challenge I am facing at the time. Within a few minutes of searching, I can usually find one or two messages that resonate with me in relation to that challenge and give me a motivational boost.

Once you have done your reading or found your motivational quotes, try to keep the main message in mind throughout the day, especially when you encounter something that might be a drain on your motivation. Let the messages help to guide you or lift you through the difficulties.

You can do the same with videos and audio books. A simple search on YouTube, iTunes or Audible will provide you with hundreds, if not thousands, of motivational videos and audio recordings.

Isaac Newton once said, "If I have seen further than others, it is by standing up the shoulders of giants."

We too, can stand upon the shoulders of giants. We can read and listen to the thoughts and messages of motivational titans from throughout the ages with little effort and at no expense.

We can cut short, or eliminate, the time spent watching shows purely for entertainment. Instead, for a few times a day, we can purposely climb up on the shoulders of those who can guide us through many of the day-to-day challenges we face as salespeople and as human beings by their experience and wisdom.

> "The key is to keep company only with people who uplift you, whose presence calls forth your best." – Epictetus

We should also strive to surround ourselves with positive people that we can share our experiences with and learn from. All the better if these people are more skilled than us at selling or at some shared interest. Surely, one of the quickest ways to improve at something is to be around people who can push or pull us to the next level.

Personally, when I see someone who does something I admire, I try to emulate that behavior. For example, I know someone that, regardless of how challenging the situation, never says anything negative. I think that that is an admirable trait and I try my best to emulate it.

On the sports field and in sales, when I see someone do something well, I try to copy what I've seen. For me, it just seems easier to copy a behavior once I have seen someone demonstrate it. It's like I'm looking for others to show me how.

In that respect, we have a chance to learn from almost everyone we encounter. And if you approach your interactions with others as an opportunity to learn from them, not only will you learn, but you will also make a positive impression on the people you are interacting with.

"Do you want to know who you are? Don't ask. Act! Action will delineate and define you." – Thomas Jefferson

---

Of course, it's not always easy. It often takes much practice, and sometimes feels impossible. But, by consciously making an effort to both learn and improve and by continually working at it step-by-step, we will get closer to our target.

Earlier I mentioned that our motivation plan should include some internal safeguards to protect us from the day-to-day challenges that may dampen our motivation. This is equally as important as looking for sources of motivation.

For starters, you need to be aware that motivation is vitally important to your success. Just that simple awareness will help you to more safely monitor and nurture your motivation.

Next, you need to become aware of any negative self talk and immediately shut it down when it starts. If you make a mistake, learn from it, promise that you will try to do better next time, and then move on.

Do NOT dwell on it. Do NOT allow yourself to attempt to make connections between the mistake that you made and some sort of personality, character, or aptitude deficiency.

"Our greatest weakness lies in giving up. The most certain way to succeed is to always try just one more time." – Thomas A. Edison

---

The reality is that a large part of our potential, our personality, our character, and our aptitudes are, regardless of our age, still undefined and open to development. So any prolonged dwelling on our perceived personal shortcomings is simply a waste of time.

Instead, when we identify opportunities for self-improvement, we should focus our thoughts on deciding which behaviors to change or adopt that will allow us to get closer our targeted outcome.

The point is that we can become the person we want to be if we make a conscious effort to do so. Alternatively, by dwelling on mistakes, we give them greater importance than they merit and we entrench ourselves in the past instead of working towards a better today.

Worry can be a big drag on motivation. It rarely helps and is usually not justified. Thus, it should be eliminated.

How do you do this? By focusing on the moment, focusing on the things you can control, and letting go of the rest.

If you are worried about tomorrow's big presentation, it's understandable. But worrying about it won't help you. Instead, take a deep breath, drop the worry, and focus your energy on preparing for and practicing your presentation.

If you are worried about whether a prospect will accept your proposal, it's also understandable. But it also won't help. Recognize that you've done your best and that you can't control everything. Take another deep breath and turn the decision over to the client. Learning to let go will reduce your worry and your fear, and will ultimately help you to protect your motivation.

If you ever feel that you are losing your motivation and the normal plan isn't getting you to the motivational place you need to be, try talking with peers, friends or family that you trust.

It's natural to feel down or encounter self-doubt from time to time. And at those times, it can be very helpful to reach out to people that we trust. So please do.

Lastly, no matter what happens, try your best to keep your enthusiasm. Your enthusiasm is what your colleagues, co-workers, clients and prospects see. It's what draws people towards you and convinces your prospects that they want to buy from you.

Simply acting with enthusiasm can often times restore our positive feelings and bring back our motivation. I repeat, even if you don't feel enthusiastic, keep acting like you are. Sometimes the actions will lead the feeling, and many times the actions will lead to positive outcomes.

In sports, often times if one team is dominating the other, the winning team's enthusiasm will increase as the game progresses. At the same time, the losing team's enthusiasm will become lower and lower as the gap in the scores widens.

However, once in a while you can witness an amazing turn around. These reversals can only take place if the losing team maintains its enthusiasm and its optimism throughout the entire game, even when they are getting beaten.

The comeback team doesn't look back and dwell on its mistakes. If anything, it learns from its errors, recommits itself, and looks only forward. It's always searching for opportunities to improve its position, believing that it still has a chance to win.

And, ultimately, even if the comeback falls short and the team loses, it's doesn't let the defeat ruin its season or dampen its enthusiasm. It works together to stay motivated, to improve, and to prepare for the next challenge.

As individuals, we should strive to do the same. Everyone has bad days. Everyone makes mistakes. And everyone suffers from misfortune. The difference is in how we choose to respond to these challenges. Do we shrink or do we grow?

I encourage you to recognize the importance that motivation plays in your success. I also encourage you to put a plan in place to protect and even increase your motivation. And, no matter what has happened, keep your enthusiasm.

If you do, good things will happen and not only will you be a top performing salesperson, but you will also lead a happier, more spontaneous and worry-free life.

Development Activity

1. Create a resource list of external motivation builders.

2. Create a list of your internal safeguards to your motivation.

3. Create a written plan for developing and protecting your motivation and check in on that plan each day.

Continual Development

"If I really want to improve my situation, I can work on the one thing over which I have control – myself." - Stephen R. Covey

The greatest performers in the world, regardless of the activity, can only achieve greatness and continue to perform at the highest levels if they spend a large amount of their time on practice. This is also true for sales superstars.

On the other hand, those who fail to put the time and effort into proper practice and preparation rarely rise above mediocre levels of performance, regardless of their natural abilities. This, too, is also true for salespeople.

Salespeople tend to be a rather independent lot. As such, many are reluctant to seek the counsel of others when it comes to developing their sales skills. In their private lives, they may take lessons for a hobby such as skiing, dancing, or learning a language. However, when it comes to the development of their professional sales and communication skills, many people are averse to coaching, self-study, and practice.

This is unfortunate, as the formula or method for developing sales skills is really no different than that of any other skill. Mastery takes commitment, time, a focus on learning the basics, and continual practice of the fundamentals mixed with the acquisition and development of increasingly higher-level skills and techniques.

If you want to learn to be a skilled golfer, skier, dancer, guitarist, public speaker, negotiator, manager, or leader, the formula is the same.

If it were your goal to become proficient in one of the abovementioned areas, wouldn't you want to find a good coach, or at least enroll in a training program or class? At a minimum, you'd purchase a good book or go online and do some research.

So why do so many salespeople avoid doing this? I believe it's because much of our ability to sell is connected with our personality and our communication skills. These are complex areas for development and are really close to the core of who we are as individuals. As such, many people are acutely sensitive to feedback about these areas.

If your tennis coach tells you that you need to work on your forehand or that your serve needs improvement, you will most likely not be offended and will simply follow the prescribed course of improvement. The same is true with negative feedback or constructive criticism of our skills related to almost any activity.

Even with more cerebral activities like playing chess or learning a computer language, most people will simply take the feedback at face value and try to improve based upon what they have been told.

However, it can be a little harder to take negative feedback if someone tells us that we need to become a better listener, or that we need to manage our time better, or that we should try to be more empathetic. Likewise, if colleague, client, or manager tells us that we should improve our presentation skills, ask more insightful questions to clients, or dress more professionally, we might try to brush off the feedback as not being important or as being out of line.

This is probably some sort of a defense mechanism designed to protect our egos and our self-esteem from critical comments about our personality or interpersonal behaviors.

Again, most people can easily take feedback about activities that aren't directly related to their core personality. However, when people receive the same type of feedback regarding communication and interpersonal skills, they tend to be more sensitive.

This is unfortunate because one of the quickest roads to self-improvement is to receive meaningful feedback from someone who both knows us and is willing to help us improve. If we allow misguided feelings of hurt or anger to cloud our view, we may miss a great opportunity to gain self-knowledge and improve our skills.

Fortunately, if you are reading this book, you have already decided that learning and personal development are important for the improvement of your sales skills. For that I commend you.

I also would like to remind you that learning theory alone isn't enough. We all need practice.

Some of the best practice opportunities come during actual client interactions. But this can only be considered practice if you are using the skills you have already developed and if you are consciously trying to practice new techniques. Effective practice also requires that you learn from client and prospect interactions and reflect on them afterwards.

For example, if you do a good job of asking questions, listening to your client and gaining an understanding of their needs, you can say that you were practicing. Likewise, if you leave the meeting and make a mental note that you need to improve the way you present your proposal or ask for information, and then develop a plan for doing so, you can call that a good practice session.

On the other hand, if simply show up and wing it, do a few things well and a few things poorly, and then run off to the next meeting without any reflection, the meeting wouldn't qualify as practice, and the chances that you will improve your skills are diminished.

Just as live performances and competitions can be great opportunities to practice and test our skills, live client interactions provide a valuable chance to practice what we have learned.

However, we shouldn't limit our practice to live client interactions. The stakes are high when we are in front of client.

This is usually not the time to attempt something for the first time.

Offline practice gives us a great opportunity to develop and improve existing and new skills in a low-pressure environment where we can get immediate feedback and keep trying until we get it right.

Presentations, for example, should be practiced with colleagues, friends or family, or in front of a mirror, or even on video before they are given to a client. The same is true of asking and responding to questions, introducing a proposal, or using negotiation tactics.

Personally, I have forced friends and family to sit through numerous presentations. I have practiced in front of the mirror. And I have video taped myself presenting and asking questions.

Some of the best practice sessions I've ever experienced took place with my sales colleagues. In one case, our company had polled sales people from around the region about the most common and most difficult questions we were asked by prospects and clients.

The company then compiled the list and sent out the top 50 questions to the sales managers in each office. The sales managers worked with their teams to compile effective answers to the questions and then returned the information the marketing department.

The best answers were selected and returned to the sales managers in each office. At that point, we practiced each question and response in pairs and in small groups. In a short time, everyone learned some important information and gained a lot confidence in their ability to respond to questions from our clients.

In another organization, the salespeople had to practice almost every element of a client meeting in small increments and as a group. For example, we would spend an hour working on how to establish the flow or agenda of the meeting. Or, we might spend time on how to present to individuals versus presenting to large groups. We would also work on elevator pitches so we could quickly and clearly tell people what services we provided and how it might benefit them.

Practicing in a group like this can be highly effective. For starters, it's typically a safe and low stress environment, i.e. the perfect place to try new skills. Secondly, watching other sales people perform and learning from what they do well or the mistakes they make can greatly accelerate the development of your own sales skills.

You can also practice on your own. This can be at the office, at home, in the car, or anywhere. I will often times mentally go through the opening of a meeting where I try to establish the meeting flow and the transition of the meeting towards a "next steps" conversation and decision while I'm in the car or on the train. By doing this, it's much easier for me to remember what to say and how to act in the meeting.

In conclusion, please remember that no matter what your current skill level is, you can rapidly improve with structured practice. I encourage you to make it part of your weekly or even daily activity targets. If you do, good things will happen.

Bonus Content I

The following is a preview chapter of the soon to be released book *The Inside Game: Sales Leadership*

Effective Use of CRM Tools

"Common sense is not so common" – Voltaire

The effective use of a Client Relationship Management (CRM) tool or system can dramatically improve the effectiveness and productivity of individual salespeople and entire sales teams.

At their best, CRM tools can be an integral part of the sales process and provide much needed assistance with time management, client communications, marketing, and reporting. However, at their worst, when they aren't used "effectively," CRM tools can be a drain on time, energy, and motivation.

This chapter will discuss how to get the most out of your CRM tool and, at the same time, how to not let your CRM tool get the most out of you. It is included in this book on sales basics because it's important for all salespeople, especially beginners, to understand how to use a CRM to make themselves more productive, and how not to be used by the CRM to make them less productive.

Most organizations, big or small, understand the importance of capturing, storing and organizing prospect and client data in a manner that makes sales and marketing activities easier to automate and execute.

The use of CRM tools to manage client and prospect information has become the norm. In fact, it's quite rare these days to work for a company that doesn't have some type CRM tool in place. These tools can range from basic databases with some sales related functionality, on up to full-blown enterprise systems that have seemingly limitless features and functions.

The key is not to buy or use the CRM tool with the most features and functions. Nor, should you try to use every single feature or function of your existing CRM system. Instead, the key is to use a CRM tool that is most appropriate for your business and to use it in the most effective manner.

What does this mean for most salespeople? Well, for starters, it means you should be able to access the CRM system from a variety of locations including the office, at home, or via a mobile device while out in the field.

You, as a salesperson, should enter the company name, contact name, title, contact details for any legitimate prospect or client that you have had contact with or expect to have contact with in the future. However, if you meet someone that clearly is not a prospect for your business, either now or in the future. Then, please, don't enter their information in your CRM tool.

Some salespeople like to demonstrate activity by entering tons of prospect and client information into the CRM. However, if the information isn't relevant or helpful for future business opportunities, then it's just wasting space in the CRM tool, and it's wasting the time of the person who is entering it.

You should always enter any meaningful client or prospect activities and communications.

What do I mean by meaningful? Well, you will have to decided that for yourself. But, as an example, writing a verbatim transcript of a casual conversation not relating your business, usually isn't meaningful.

You can, if you like, write a short summary so you can remember and refer to key points in the future. Or, you may just make a note that the conversation occurred and bullet point any important information.

Likewise, spending the time and energy to input an entire company profile of a low-grade prospect usually isn't an effective use of your time or the storage space in your CRM tool. Remember, you are getting paid based upon sales results not data entry. So just enter what's essential and then move on.

Definitely, input the results of face-to-face meetings, conference and phone calls. But again, just input the meat and potatoes that are relevant to your business. You should forget about all the trimmings, like who said what about today's weather.

Your CRM system should be set up to capture past client communications and prompt future responses. So, for example, if a prospect requests that you call them on the first day of the next month, you should be able to set that as an "alert" in your CRM system.

Then, when that time and date roles around, your CRM tool will send an alert to whatever computer or mobile device you are using reminding you to call that prospect and giving you their contact number. Alerts can be used to remind you to make calls, send emails, deliver proposals, and attend meetings.

Your CRM tool should also capture all client and prospect emails so that you can easily refer to information in past communications.

Lastly, your CRM tool should include a calendar option that allows you to plan your daily activities and then serves you the relevant information related to each activity.

For example, if you are going to spend two hours calling prospects, it would be ideal if your CRM tool would show that on your calendar and then display the names and contact numbers of the prospects you plan to call. And then, after each call, you should be able to easily enter any additional information related to that prospect or set future activity reminders.

As a general rule I would limit the type and amount of data to be entered into a CRM tool to only those that data that can be used to directly improve the efficiency of the individual salespeople or that may be used to generate leads or retain clients by marketing type activities.

For example, if the marketing department wanted to send a targeted communication regarding a special offer to a specific group of prospects, they should be able to use the CRM tool to do this. However, if they don't have the contact information or if they can't filter by prospect type, they won't be able to use the CRM tool, or the data stored in the CRM tool to conduct the marketing campaign.

Here's where it can get to be a little tricky. Some organizations will ask or require that their salespeople input and continually update all types of extra information. This may include complex company profile information that can be used by the marketing department to more effectively target their campaigns.

In these situations, the sales team ends up doing the work, i.e. the data input, for the marketing team so that the marketing team can be more effective. This may, in turn, help the sales force, as they may benefit from receiving additional leads or improved client communications.

However, if salespeople are spending too much time on data entry, they won't be out selling. With that in mind, it's important that a balance be struck between the time spent on this activity and benefits received.

In my opinion, the worst misuse of CRM tools comes from some of the reporting requirement that many organizations require.

For example, it's reasonable for organizations to track sales related activities such as meetings held and proposals delivered. But, if the activity tracking is too detailed, you will again be forced to spend too much time on data entry.

In fact, if organizations focus too much on activity recording and tracking, you will see salespeople who focus their efforts on activity recording in the CRM tool, to make themselves look productive when, in fact, they might not be producing sufficient revenues.

As a sales manager, I would always try to minimize all reporting requirements related to activity. The CRM should be used to automate, or semi-automate, the reporting of many key metrics such as the number of prospects a salesperson has, the number of clients, the number of meetings held, proposals delivered, and the total value of outstanding proposals.

It may even be reasonable to enter information regarding the potential revenue from specific prospects and clients, and expected date to start new opportunities, and the likelihood of that specific opportunity to be come to fruition.

Where things can easily out of hand is when management starts to request information that is either too detailed or requires too much time to collect or enter. The most common example is in when detailed revenue projections are required for prospects.

I've seen reporting requirements that require monthly revenue projections reaching 24 months into the future for all prospects. Even worse, the projections needed to be linked to a specific service with detailed information about how that service was going to be priced and delivered.

None of this information would help the actual salespeople find new prospects or close deals. And, since the data entered was merely projections based upon the opinions of the individual salespeople, or what those salespeople wanted to show as their potential revenues, the benefit to the senior management team was minimal. It did, on the other hand, require hours and hours of data entry.

To make matters even worse, many CRM tools can be quite complex. So, not only are salespeople required to spend their time entering data, they must first learn how to use the CRM tool. For more complicated tools this can again require hours and hours of time.

And, every time there is an additional reporting requirement that can't be automated from existing data, more training and more data entry is required.

Now, as an individual salesperson, you may not have much say in what CRM tool is used and how your organization requires you to use it. However, you can choose to spend your time using the tool in the manner that helps you to sell more. All other activities should be done in a minimalist manner.

In short, do what is required, but focus your efforts on things that help you generate more revenues. At the end of the day, in most organizations, that is what really counts.

A CRM Nightmare

I once consulted for a rapidly growing company that did direct clients sales via the Internet and enterprise sales via an international sales team located in six cities around the world.

Just before I came aboard, the company had decided that it needed a new CRM system. This decision was driven by both the management, who wanted greater insight into the activity of the sales team and the value of the enterprise sales pipeline, and the sales team, who wanted an easier way to manage prospect and client information and communications.

The company purchased the required number of licenses of the leading web-based CRM tool. At that point everyone was very excited to start using the tool. And, that is also exactly the same point where things started to go wrong.

For starters, the company couldn't decide who would be responsible for the implementation of the tool.

Some executives argued that since the CRM tool was a type of software, that it should be managed by the IT department. Others argued that since the data would be used by the marketing team, that that team should manage the implementation. A third group argued that the sales team would be using the CRM tool the most and thus, they should manage it.

In the end, the company had to hire a CRM administrator who was responsible for collecting the requirements of the different users and then setting up the system in a manner that would effectively allow for the capture and dissemination of that information. This step took time and, of course, additional resources.

When the system was finally ready for use by the company's salespeople, it was almost impossible for them to figure out how to use the system. Simple things like how to set up a prospect, or how to differentiate between a "prospect" and an "opportunity," were not clear.

The CRM administrator was then required to give training sessions on a variety of topics. And, since the sales force was located in several different time zones, the training had to be repeated many times. Furthermore, whenever a person missed a training session or when a new salesperson joined the team, the training had to be repeated yet again.

The salespeople were also required to enter complex financial projections for all prospects for a 2-year period. As the company sold several different services, each with its' own pricing system, the method of entry was complex and time consuming. And, at the end of the day, the projections weren't very accurate and provided little real value to the senior management.

The final result was that the CRM tool cost more than anticipated, was too complex, and took up a lot of valuable sales time. Worse yet, instead of being seen as a helpful tool provided by management to support the sales team's efforts, the CRM tool was considered to be an intrusive hassle that delivered little value. It ended up affecting both performance and motivation in a negative manner.

A CRM Home Run

I once worked as a regional GM for a B2B media company that had, in my opinion, an ideal implementation of a CRM system that provided the appropriate type of sales support and management reporting and wasn't a time drag on the sales force.

To start with the company limited each salesperson to a 150 prospects. In order to claim a prospect as theirs, a salesperson would have to create an entry for that prospect in the CRM tool. And, to keep the prospect, the salesperson would either have to convert the prospect to a paying customer, or at least have had at least one face-to-face meeting with the prospect in the last six months, and have logged that meeting in the CRM tool.

This provided the necessary motivation to log relevant activity in the system. It also helped that the CRM tool's user interface was very intuitive. That is, users could easily create new prospects and would be prompted to enter the necessary information.

When entering prospect and client information, the salespeople would be offered an opportunity to set alerts for future activity. They would also be prompted to enter an expected revenue amount for the prospect over the next 12 months.

By capturing prospect information, meeting activity and notes, and revenue expectations, the company management could monitor the growth of the sales pipeline in terms of number of new prospects and in terms of future revenue expectations. For many companies, these are the most important indicators of future sales performance.

Top-performing salespeople were provided the additional support of a sales coordinator who would enter any necessary information into the CRM tool on behalf of the salesperson, freeing up more time for client facing activities. This also improved motivation and performance.

The salespeople in this company really appreciated the CRM tool, as it made them more productive and was easy to use. The marketing department used the CRM to send monthly emails and highly targeted bi-monthly mailings to the prospects, focusing most of their efforts on the higher-grade prospects. And, since the management team was able to monitor sales activity and pipeline growth, they were happy as well.

In companies where there is no CRM tool in place, you may have to create your own. This can be done by creating a simple Excel spreadsheet, or even going old school and recording everything in a notebook or planner to record activities and create reminders for future events.

The point is that, you need to have a system to record prospect and client information and communications. You also need to have some way to be reminded about future activities.

In conclusion, you should definitely use some type of CRM tool as they are proven productivity increasers. However, whatever tool, system, or process you use, make sure you focus your time and effort on entering only the data that is relevant to your future success.

Bonus Content II

Podcast Transcript One: *www.theinsidegame-sales.com*

How to become a top performing sales person and enjoy every step of the way!

Hello everyone!

Welcome to Mark Shriner's The Inside Game of Sales, where you will learn how to become a top performing salesperson and enjoy every step of the way.

This is Mark Shriner, and I will be your host for this session of The Inside Game.

I'd like to start today's program with a couple of simple questions?

Do you want to become a top performing salesperson? Would you like to double or triple your commissions in the next year?

Would you like to enjoy every aspect of sales and all the steps to becoming a top performer?

If you answered yes, to any of these questions, congratulations you are the right place.

Because that's exactly what you are going to learn to do.

If you answered yes, and you are serious about these goals, then for the next 10 minutes, put away your phone, stop checking your email, forget about Facebook, and do you yourself a giant favor, just concentrate on this podcast.

If you do, I can promise that in 10 minutes time, you will have learned one the of the key secrets of top performers.

Alright, let's begin. I'm going to start off with a story.

A few years ago, one of my colleagues, Tom, was offered a country manager position. Now Tom was one these great guys that you love to work with. I mean he would literally run through walls to get the job done. He brought a massively positive can do attitude to whatever he was doing.

This country manager role was a huge opportunity for Tom. But he was reluctant to try for it, because the job involved selling. Tom was worried that since he lacked sales experience and in his words, "didn't know anything about sales," that he wouldn't be able to do that part of the job.

Now keep in mind that Tom had always been in an operational role. He had absolutely no sales experience.

Well, Tom came to me for advice. I could easily see that he badly wanted the job. But I could also see that he was worried.

I told Tom, not to worry, because he already had the most important ingredient to becoming a great salesperson, a great attitude. I told him, "With an attitude like yours, sales will not only be easy, it will be fun."

Still, in spite of my reassurances, Tom wasn't completely sold on the idea. Others had warned him that sales could be really difficult and challenging.

So I told Tom, if he were willing to be coached by me, I could personally guarantee that he would become a top performer and enjoy the work. Again, I knew that I could say that, because Tom already had the most important ingredient for success in sales, a great attitude.

Well, Tom agreed, he took the new role, followed my program for sale success, and by the end of the year, not only had he become a great Country Manager, he became a great salesperson.

The training was baptism by fire. Within a couple of days, I had him on the phone cold calling senior executives to book meetings.

Many people would've been too worried about what would happen when they call, or how people would respond, and might have decided to just give up at that point.

But, Tom stayed positive and made the calls.

He had his ups and downs. You know, people said "no" and some people weren't so nice.
But he had such a great attitude that in the first hour of calling he had booked three high level meetings, one of which was later converted to a client.

After that his confidence soared, and he was like this pit bull, attacking his daily sales training and activities. He didn't worry about what people would say, or about rejection, or any of the other needless things that get a lot of wannabe salespeople down. He focused on his actions and activities. He just kept doing what needed to be done.

In the end it paid off, mostly because of his great attitude, and partially, I'd like to think, because of my coaching. ;-) But the reality, is, Tom wouldn't have gotten off of first base without his great attitude and ability to focus on the things that he could control.

So why is attitude so important?

Well for starters it's one of the few things in sales that you can control. And it's the one thing that determines how you will approach all the other aspects of sales.

I mean, in sales there are so many things that are out of our control. If you focus on those things, and let those things affect your mood, you will be on one huge never ending emotional rollercoaster.

It's like every time someone says no, or maybe, or treats you badly, or buys from your competitor, it can be like a massive body blow, if you let it, or if you think those things are important.

But people like Tom know that's a waste of time and energy.

You can't control whether a prospect says yes or no. So why worry about it?

You can't control the competition. You can't control the market, or your product development team, or your boss. At best you might be able to mildly influence a few of these things. But for the most part, it's a sucker's game to even think about them.

Trying to control those things is like trying to control the weather. It's going to rain, or be cloudy, or be sunny, and there's nothing you can do about it. You can't change it.

So, why not forget about the weather and focus on things you can control?

That is what top performers do. They know that the battle will be won or lost based upon what's going on in their mind and with their habits and behaviors. They know that to win the battle and the war that they need to focus on the things that they can control.

Your winning attitude starts there, a conscious decision to stop worrying about things you can't control and to focus on things you can control like your attitude, your activity, your professional development, and the way you manage your time.

But it all starts with your attitude.

You might be thinking, how the heck can we control our attitude?

Well, I have to say, it's heck of lot easier to change your attitude than it is to change your company, your market, or the competitiveness of your product.

And, in addition to being controlled by you, a changed attitude can have immediate effects on your performance and those around you.

So, how does this process start?

Well, it's going to sound way too simple, but the change in attitude starts simply by choosing to focus on the things you can control, and think positive thoughts about those things.

So for example, what are your thoughts about cold calling?

Is cold calling tough? Well, it is, if you say it is!

Is it easy? Again, it's up to you!

Hard or easy are just ways for you to explain your feelings about some activity.

Why don't we just throw the whole hard or easy discussion out the window?

Let's look at the activity in a more rationale manner.

Is cold calling, an activity you can control? YES!
Will it help you find clients? Yes!
Will it help you improve your communication skills?
Will you learn about the market, about people? Will you get more meetings? Will other good things happen? Yes! Yes! Yes!

So who cares if it's hard or easy? Just do it.

Thinking about it in those terms of hard or easy makes no sense. But that's exactly what a lot of underperforming salespeople do.

The same can be said about going to networking events, or meeting with prospects, practicing your presentations, getting up early, working late, sending more emails, making more calls and all those things that will get you more deals and help you to improve your skills.

You may feel they are hard or easy. But the reality is they are all things that you can control, and they are all things that will benefit you, and help you to become a better salesperson.

Or, you could choose to hang out by the water cooler trying to convince your colleague and yourself, that you have a tough job. You could worry about the competition, or the results of upcoming meeting. You could waste your energy on things that are out of your control.

But, what will that get you? Absolutely nothing that's helpful.

You know, as the saying goes, "Whether you think you can or you think you can't, you are right!"

Well, top performers choose to think they can! And then they do!

The doing reinforces their confidence and their skills. This leads to success, which leads to more confidence and the whole darn thing starts to snowball.

That's how a guy with no sales experience could become a great salesperson in less than a year. That's how you can take control of your business, your development, and the amount of money you make.

But you don't have to take my word for it.

Ralph Waldo Emerson, he said, "A man is what he thinks about all day long."

And, William James, the famous American philosopher and psychologist said "Human beings can alter their lives by altering their attitudes of mind."

Let me say that again, "Human beings can alter their lives by altering their attitudes of mind."

So, get your attitude right, and success will follow!

Now of course, in addition to getting their attitudes right, there are many more things that top performers do. And, yes, we will be discussing these and more in later podcasts of The Inside Game.

In the meantime, if you are serious about becoming a top performer, if you want to sell more and make more, then get over to www.theinsidegame-sales.com and register for a free copy of "The 10 Secrets of Sales Superstars."

This 1-page, easy to read, very powerful article will quickly get you on the road to becoming a sales superstar.

Remember, www.theinsidegame-sales.com

Until next time,

Happy Sales from Mark Shriner and The Inside Game.

Bonus Content III

Podcast Transcript Two: www.theinsidegame-sales.com

The Quickest Way to Become a Sales Superstar; Walk the Walk

Hello Everyone!

Welcome to Mark Shriner's The Inside Game of Sales, where you will learn how to become a top performing salesperson and enjoy every step of the way.

This is Mark Shriner, and I will be your host for this session of The Inside Game.

Today you are going to learn the quickest, fastest, and easiest way to become a sales superstar.
This technique is absolutely THE SECRET to becoming a top performer. So listen up!

Alright, I like stories, and I have a good one for today's podcast.

A few years ago, I was coaching a salesperson named Paul. And, at that time, Paul happened to be responsible for sales in a particular city.

Now Paul had been in sales for about eight years, had always performed at just above average levels, and was known to be a really likeable person. He had told his manager and me that he wanted to perform at a higher level but just wasn't sure how to get there.

So I asked Paul if I could go with him on a few sales calls, and he agreed.

Just prior to the first meeting I asked Paul "So, what's our goal for this meeting?" He answered, "To introduce our company."

Well as the meeting started Paul spent a good deal of time developing rapport with the person we were meeting. This was Paul's strength and was where he felt most comfortable.

But, when it came time to transition into a more business-focused discussion, Paul started to stumble. He clearly wasn't comfortable making the transition.

And then when he started to introduce his company he pulled out some black and white copies of a power point presentation that weren't bound together. He then tried to try to organize all the papers in front of the prospect, which of course, was pretty of awkward.

Anyway, Paul did manage to go through his presentation. But, he did it line by line, not really adding any color to the content, or asking any questions to check his prospect's understanding.

The prospect then asked Paul if he would like an overview of his company's needs. Paul said "sure." And, so the person we were meeting gave us an overview of their operations and their requirements.

During that time, Paul was attentive, however, he didn't ask many questions, and didn't take notes. As the meeting wound down, Paul thanked the prospect for his time and both parties agreed to keep in touch.

When we left, I asked Paul how he felt about the meeting. He said it was quite positive. When I asked about next steps, Paul said he would touch base with the prospect in a few weeks.

Now this pattern repeated itself over the next few meetings. At that point, I decided that we needed to talk.

Can you guess what we talked about?

Well instead of directly pointing out the areas where I believed Paul could improve, I asked Paul a couple of simple questions.

I said "Paul imagine there are two salespeople. Average Sales Paul who makes $ 75,000 a year, and Superstar Sales Paul who makes $ 250,000 a year or even more."

"Which would you like to be? And, which one are you?"

Paul, answered, "Well, I'm the first person, but would definitely like to be the superstar salesperson."

So I said, "Paul if you want be sales superstar, you first gotta act like a sales superstar!"

He gave me a puzzled look and said, "Well how can I act like a superstar, if I'm not a superstar?"

And that question, that false reasoning, ladies and gentlemen, is the number one reason most salespeople fail to achieve their full potential.

I explained to Paul, "If you act like an average salesperson, you will always be average. But if you want to be a superstar then start doing the things a superstar does. In short, start acting like superstar."

To make it easier for Paul to understand this concept in relation to his own performance, I asked him several questions. I'd like to you to listen to these questions, and think how you would reply, or act during a prospect meeting.

1. Would a superstar go into a meeting with a clearly defined goal that included next steps and moving the sale process forward?

2. Would a superstar spend time to develop rapport?

3. Would a superstar be confident in transitioning the meeting from rapport building to the business conversation?

4. Would a superstar have neatly bound handouts to support the introduction of his company?

5. Would a superstar take notes during the meeting?

6. Would a superstar ask intelligent and relevant questions to the prospect?

7. Would a superstar end the meeting by getting some type of commitment from the prospect to move the process forward?

Paul answered yes to all of these questions. How about you? How many of these questions did you answer yes to?

And, more importantly, how many of these things do you actually do?

Paul, had only really been doing the rapport building. Everything, he'd had been skipping or doing in a half-hearted manner.

So told Paul, that if he wanted to be a superstar he should simply start doing those other six things that he answered "yes" to. Of course, in reality, there are more than just these six. But, for the time being, we decided to focus just on these.

We put together a plan for each of the items on the list and Paul started to implement these items in all his meetings. To do so, and to keep him on track, Paul had a checklist that he called his "Walk the

Walk" list. This was basically the list of behaviors related to acting like, or" walking the walk," of a superstar.

There was an immediate change in Paul's performance. He started to make more progress with more prospects.

He didn't master all the skills and actions at once. However, within a few weeks he had improved greatly on most of them, and the difference in Paul was amazing.

Paul was going into meetings with a sense of purpose and direction. His prospects could feel his confidence. And, since he was now taking a lot of the guesswork out of the meetings, Paul started to actually enjoy the business side of the meetings much more.

This in turn led to increased confidence and then again better results and more enjoyment.

Over the next year, Paul almost doubled his sales volume and told me that couldn't believe how simple it had been to start performing at a higher level.

So what's the lesson we can learn from this story?

It's easy, the lesson is, "You are as you do."

You ever heard of Aristotle? Well ole Aristotle, he said, "We are what we repeatedly do. Excellence, then, is not an act, but a habit."

Therefore, if you want to be a pro athlete, a professional musician, a great businessperson, then act like one. Spend the necessary time on practice, preparation, planning, training, and performance.
If you want to be a sales superstar then, likewise, invest the effort in doing all the things that top performers do.

Now lets take a step back to see how that relates to the six items we mentioned earlier.

Sales superstars go into every meeting with a clearly defined goal or set of objectives that will somehow move the sales process forward and closer to the conclusion of a deal.

An additional objective for every meeting is to further develop the trust of the person you are meeting.

Developing rapport is always a good idea, even with people who don't like to chit-chat. Because you need to connect on a personal level with your prospects and clients. This was Paul's specialty.

However, at some point in the meeting you also need to transition into the business discussion and start moving towards your objectives. So work on your transition techniques.

When it comes to sales support materials top performers always make sure they have everything prepared in advance. This can include handouts and power point presentations. And, if you are going to use a computer, definitely make sure that you bring all the necessary cables, plugs and adapters.

I've seen too many presentation derailed because the salesperson couldn't connect to the LCD, or the LAN, or because they couldn't charge their computer's battery.

When it comes to the prospect sharing information with you, ALWAYS take notes. Doing so sends the message that you are listening to, and value, what the person is saying.

And this brings us the to topic of getting our prospects to share information with us.

You need to think about the questions you will ask in advance. Because these questions are both an opportunity for you learn about your prospect's situation, and also an opportunity for you demonstrate your professional expertise.

For example, if you ask a real basic question such as "can you please tell me about your business?" your prospect might get the idea that you haven't researched their company or aren't familiar with their industry.

However, if you were to ask a more complex question, you can demonstrate your knowledge about industry trends and solutions.

For example, you could say, "Many of our clients are concerned about reducing costs and are considering to outsource non-core activities. What are your thoughts on this topic?"

By asking a more complex question like this, I can show that I'm working with other companies in the industry and am aware of solutions that they are implementing.

Lastly, a superstar would never end a meeting without getting some type of commitment to move the process forward. If you don't get this, you risk having the whole process put on hold and losing all forward momentum.

Now these are some examples of walking the walk of top performing salespeople. Of course, there are many other sales related behaviors we could discuss. And, we will in future podcasts of The Inside Game.

But for now, lets conclude with this.

If you want to become a top performer, if you want to be sale superstar, then, look around, look at the top performers, observe the behaviors that help them to succeed and immediately start to adopt the ones that are appropriate for you.

It's as simple as that.

Make a conscious decision to take responsibility for your performance and success. Start acting like the sales superstar that you want to be.

If you do, you will quickly become a top performing salesperson and enjoy every step of the way.

And, if you are serious about becoming a top performer, if you want to sell more and make more, then get over to www.theinsidegame-sales.com and register for a free copy of "The 10 Secrets of Sales Superstars."

This short easy to read article will quickly get you on the road to becoming a sales superstar.

Remember, www.theinsidegame-sales.com.

Until next time,

Happy Sales from Mark Shriner and The Inside Game.

Bonus Content IV

TEN SECRETS OF SALES SUPERSTARS

---

1. Understanding CLIENT NEEDS is INFINITELY more important than talking about your product, service, or company.

SO ASK QUESTIONS, LISTEN, AND ASK MORE QUESTIONS. WHEN YOU ARE DONE, RECAP WHAT YOU HAVE LEARNED TO YOUR CLIENT TO SEE IF YOU HAVE UNDERSTOOD THEM CORRECTLY. AND, REMEMBER, EMPATHY IS A LEADING INDICATOR OF SUCCESS.

2. Product and Knowledge and Belief are critical ingredients in being able introduce your product or service in a confident, enthusiastic and professional manner.

SO STUDY YOUR PRODUCT, LEARN ALL POSSIBLE APPLICATIONS, BENEFITS, FEATURES, COMPETITIVE ADVANTAGES AND DISADVANTAGES

3. Before you get the sale, you have to EARN your client's TRUST.

SO ACT PROFESSIONALY, BE ON TIME, MAKE AND KEEP COMMITMENTS. BE A RESOURCE TO YOUR CLIENTS BY PROVIDING UNBIASED INFORMATION THAT HELPS YOUR CLIENTS TO MAKE DECISIONS OR OPERATE MORE EFFICIENTLY IN THEIR JOBS. ACCELERATE THE TRUST ACQUISITION PROCESS BY GETTING INTRODUCED BY SOMEONE YOUR CLIENT ALREADY TRUSTS.

4. ATTITUDE trumps APTITUDE 9 times out of 10.

SO, STAY POSITIVE AND FOCUSED AND NEVER, EVER, EVER GIVE UP!

5. Your MOST valuable asset is your TIME.

SO, PLAN YOUR WEEKLY SCHEDULE IN ADVANCE. DON'T WASTE TIME TRYING FIGURE OUT WHAT TO DO NEXT. WHEN IN DOUBT, STICK WITH YOUR SCHEDULE. PUT THE MOST IMPORTANT ACTIVITIES ON YOUR SCHEDULE FIRST AND DON'T LET ANYTHING INTERFERE WITH THOSE ACTIVITIES.

6. ACTIVITY leads to RESULTS. Inactivity leads to NO where, fast!

SO, FOCUS ON ACTIVITIES THAT LEAD TO SALES OR MOVE YOU CLOSER TO THE SALE. GET MEETINGS, DELIVER PROPOSALS, AND CALL AND MEET MORE PROSPECTS. TRACK YOUR ACTIVITIES AND KEEP SCORE. IF YOU DO, THE SCORE WILL GET BETTER AND YOUR SALES WILL INCREASE.

7. ALWAYS be LEARNING

SO, ALWAYS BE LEARNING! AFTER EVERY CLIENT INTERACTION, OR ANY SALES RELATED ACTIVITY, ASK YOURSELF WHAT YOU CAN DO TO IMPROVE. IF YOU MAKE A MISTAKE, DON'T GET DOWN ON YOURSELF, TREAT IT AS A LEARNING OPPORTUNITY AND MOVE ON. READ BOOKS ABOUT SALES, SELF MOTIVATION, EFFECTIVE COMMUNICATION, AND TIME MANAGEMENT. KNOW YOUR PRODUCT. ALWAYS BE LEARNING!

8. Warm LEADS are IMPORTANT

SO, CULTIVATE LEADS FROM MULTIPLE SOURCES INCLUDING EXISTING CLIENTS, COLLEAGUES, FRIENDS, AND FAMILY. GET INVOLVED AND BE VISIBLE WITH RELEVANT ORGANIZATIONS. BE KNOWN AS A SUBJECT MATTER EXPERT. USE SOCIAL MEDIA. GAIN THE SUPPORT OF YOUR MARKETING TEAM. WHENEVER

YOU RECEIVE A LEAD, BE SURE TO FOLLOW UP, AND NOT ONLY THANK THE SOURCE OF THE LEAD, BUT KEEP THEM UPDATED ON YOUR PROGRESS.

9. Have a Game PLAN for each client meeting or interaction

SO, KNOW WHAT YOU WANT TO ACHIEVE IN THE MEETING AND HAVE A PLAN FOR GUIDING THE MEETING TOWARDS YOUR GOAL. IN ADDITION TO YOUR STATED OBJECTIVE, EVERY MEETING SHOULD ALSO ACCOMPLISH THE NON-STATED BUT EQUALLY IMPORTANT PARALLEL GOALS OF MOVING YOU CLOSER TO THE SALE AND DEVELOPING THE TRUST OF YOUR CLIENT OR PROSPECT.

10. People LIKE to buy from people that they LIKE

SO, BE LIKEABLE. BE A GOOD EMPATHETIC LISTENER. BE A PERSON THAT YOUR CLIENT TRUSTS AND APPRECIATES. IF YOU DO, GOOD THINGS WILL HAPPEN.

The above ten "secrets" really aren't secrets at all. They are actually more akin to fundamentals. So, why are they called "secrets?" It's because the majority of salespeople have either not learned them, have forgotten them, or chose not to remember them.

Therefore, this list is designed to be used as daily prompt to those sales professionals who want to be continually reminded of the key ingredients to becoming a top performer.

If that is you, then I encourage you to take a few minutes each day to read through this list and ask yourself how you are performing in relation to each item. This simple act will quickly lead to awareness, improvement, and sales success.

Happy Hunting!

Mark Shriner
www.theinsidegame-sales.com

Acknowledgments

This book is based on lessons learned during my more than 20 years experience as a salesperson, sales manager, executive, sales trainer, and leadership coach, in the U.S. and throughout the Asia Pacific region. As such, I need to first and foremost, acknowledge and thank the companies, colleagues, clients, and individuals I have worked with or coached during those years. The list is too long to include here, but you know who you are. My greatest lessons have come from you. Thank you!

I owe a special debt of gratitude Brandon Smith, Oscar Wu, and Douglas Shih. You all three taught me a tremendous amount about sales, but also mentored me through challenging times.

I'd also like to recognize Peter Galante at Innovative Language Learning for giving me both guidance and encouragement to pursue my goals. Thank you!

Lea Saguisag Jusi, you are a great friend and an equally excellent editor. Thank you!

Finally, I'd like to thank my family starting with my mother for being a great listener and, through her own success, an inspiration to her two sons. Mom, your attitude is simply amazing. Thanks to my brother Matthew for always taking my calls, listening to my rants, and giving me advice as needed. That's how we're gonna gettem!

Most importantly, I'd like to thank my wife Sunny and our three wonderful boys - Markus, Makai, and Lukas – for their love, support, energy and music. No one could ever ask for more.

About the Author

Mark Shriner has been a top-performing salesperson, executive, and sales trainer for over 20 years. He has successfully sold both B2B and B2C services in the U.S. and throughout Asia, and has worked in a variety of positions including sales director, vice president global sales, country manager, managing director, and CEO Asia Pacific. In every position, Mark has used the methods and techniques outlined in this book to help him and his teams become top performers.

Having earned several internationally recognized coaching certifications, including the Marshall Goldsmith Stakeholder Centered Coaching certificate, Mark conducts workshops and customized sales and motivational programs for individuals and companies in the U.S., Europe, and Asia.

To find out how Mark can help you or your organization immediately increase sales and become top performers contact:

admin@theinsidegame-sales.com
www.theinsidegam-sales.com

www.ingramcontent.com/pod-product-compliance
Lightning Source LLC
Chambersburg PA
CBHW071416170526
45165CB00001B/291